TRAVELS ON FOOT THROUGH THE ISLAND OF CEYLON

TRAVELS ON FOOT THROUGH THE ISLAND OF CEYLON

J. HAAFNER

TRANSLATED FROM THE DUTCH

Published by

Facsimile Publisher
12 Pragati Market
Ashok Vihar, Ph-2
Delhi-110052
facsimilepublisher.com

Distribution Network
gyanbooks.com
India, USA, Canada, UK, Australia, France

ISBN : 978-93-5324-505-4 (HB)
First Published, London, 1821

2nd Impression 2020

Printed at: Gyan Press, Delhi.

Travels on Foot Through the Island of Ceylon
Author: J. Haafner

TRAVELS

ON FOOT THROUGH THE ISLAND

OF

CEYLON.

WITH ENGRAVINGS.

By J. HAAFNER.

TRANSLATED FROM THE DUTCH.

LONDON.

PRINTED FOR SIR RICHARD PHILLIPS AND Co.

BRIDE COURT, BRIDGE STREET.

1821.

TRAVELS

IN THE

ISLAND OF CEYLON.*

CHAPTER I.

Escape from Madras by Tranquebar to Ceylon—Arrival at Jaffnapatnam—Manner of living—Gulf of Catchaï.

HAVING been a prisoner of war for a considerable time in the city of Madras, I found it impossible to remain any longer a witness to the misery that prevailed in it, and being in great danger of also perishing in the general famine, I resolved to make my escape to the Danish settlement of Tranquebar, where I soon after arrived in an open and leaky boat. My first intention was to remain here and wait the issue of the war, but I soon found that notwithstanding the neutrality of the place, it was as much exposed to the rapacity of the contending powers as others; and, contrary to my expectations, provisions were scarce and extremely dear. As my finances in such a place would have speedily been exhausted, I resolved to leave Tranquebar as soon as possible, and seek a safer and cheaper asylum. But where should I find shelter—to the English I neither would nor durst return; the Dutch were completely ruined, the English had taken and destroyed all their settlements on the coast of *Orixa* and *Coromandel*. The island of Ceylon was the only place of security

* A modern Dutch account of Ceylon, now that island is become an English colony, cannot fail to be interesting to English readers, independently of the curious facts and singular adventures detailed by the writer. The value of the work is also enhanced by the consideration that the works published describe districts bordering on the sea coast only, or of general statistics.

from famine and war; and I could reach it in little more than a day, when I should find myself once more among my countrymen. Without further deliberation, then, I left the coast, and, accompanied by a young and amiable female, I arrived safe at *Jaffnapatnam*, after making several narrow escapes.

During my long residence on the coast of Coromandel, I had often wished to see this fine town, and now having it full before me, I must confess, that its situation and appearance far exceeded the high expectations I had formed. On the morning of our arrival, the sun was just rising in all his splendour; before me at a short distance lay Jaffnapatnam, in a wide amphitheatre, with its white houses intersected with groves and gardens, which, with the dark green gigantic palm and cocoa-trees, produced a most charming and enchanting effect.

I found here many friends and old acquaintances who had fled from the misery and famine which had desolated the coast. Among others, to my great joy, I met with Mr. Templin, formerly overseer of the coopers in the settlement at *Nagapatnam*. When that establishment was taken, the English plundered him of almost all his effects; he had fled to Jaffnapatnam with the little he could save, and purchased a garden planted with cocoa and arrack-trees, the produce of which supported his numerous family. His garden was without the city, and I had the good fortune to obtain one near to it, from Mr. Schröter, secretary of the police, with whom I became acquainted on the day I arrived, and who kindly offered me the use of it.

Here, then, I lived in tranquillity and peace, free from all care, grief, and vexation. I can scarcely recollect a period in the whole course of my life, in which I was so completely happy, so truly content as then at Jaffnapatnam. And no wonder; I possessed all that can render a man happy in this world. I had property enough to enable me to live in a liberal manner, and in worthy Templin I had an honest man for my friend. I had always considered independence as the greatest gift of heaven—no one had now the command over me, I had nobody to fear, and was completely my own lord and master. I loved a retired life, and in this also my wish was gratified. The house in which I lived had a grove of rustling palm and cocoa-trees behind, and before a flower-garden and shrubbery. I was besides blest with the society of *Anna*, whose heart I possessed without any mixture of self-interest, and thus my days passed away, like the current of a clear brook among borders of flowers.

It would be too tedious to describe the various amusements in which I passed my time with my friends, or the numerous parties of pleasure to which I was invited to make excursions to the surrounding villages. Our favourite place of resort was *Neloer*, the situation of which is enchanting beyond description. The inhabitants of Jaffnapatnam frequently form large parties of men, women, and children, and remain in the village for several days, to enjoy the beauty of its scenery, and the pleasures it affords. But what shall I say of the other amusements which made the time pass away so delightfully—of my wanderings with *Anna* to this or the other distant and solitary spot, when we spent the whole day together—amused ourselves like children, and were, like them, happy. Sometimes we went to the nearest village, where some good woman prepared our repast of rice and kerry, while our drink was the delicious cocoa-nut, or fresh palm wine. With regret we saw the darkness approach and force us to return to our dwelling.

My morning and evening walks to the delightful bay of *Catchaï** must not be passed over in silence. At four o'clock, before sun-rise I set out, while *Anna* prepared breakfast for my return. I took my way through the groves of palm and cocoa-trees, while all nature around me seemed to rejoice. The early crows rose by hundreds from the trees, and with ceaseless cawing skimmed around in confused and eccentric circles. The Avontrow,† spreading his broad pinions and leaving his high place of rest, mounted slowly to the sky to greet the approaching sun. I at last took my stand on the shore of the bay of *Catchaï*, and beheld the king of day rising with slow and majestic steps from the blue waters. Light clouds with gilded edges surround him; every moment his beams increase in strength, and the dew-covered plants already feel the influence of his cherishing rays. But towards evening, when the sun had almost finished his course, and the cooling sea-breeze had tempered the heat of the day, this spot had new charms for me, and seldom did I fail, accompanied by Anna, to visit those delightful shores. The evening breeze rustling among the high tops of the palm-trees, and the rippling of the waves on the sandy beech, flocks of wild ducks, divers, and all kinds of water fowl, rising from the sea, and repairing to their haunts on the land; tortoises, (with which the shore was covered) creeping to their holes, the long-legged, snow-white, *koukous*‡ hastening to their nests on the high trees—all an-

* A bay or gulf that divides the peninsula of Jaffnapatnam from the rest of Ceylon.

† The mountain eagle.

‡ The *koukou* is a kind of stork, which agrees with the description given of the Egyptian ibis. It is a lonely bird, and lives only on fish, frogs, &c. Its step is stately and slow, and sometimes it stands immoveable on one foot with its shoulders drawn in, and its beak resting on its breast, in a meditating posture. The Indians have the same veneration for the koukou as the Dutch have for the stork, because it clears the land of reptiles. It often endeavours to surprise the eel among the mud, but sometimes instead of the slippery prey, it disturbs the haunt

nounced the approach of night; while the wild geese, in long ranks arriving from every quarter, closed the varying scenes of the day.

CHAPTER II.

Inclination to travel—Secret wish—Unexpected gratification of it—My fellow-travellers—The Oppa.

I HAD lived in this manner at Jaffnapatnam several months, in undisturbed repose, when an unexpected occurrence all at once awoke in me an inclination to travel, and forced me from the abode of peace and happiness.

The love of travelling is an unfortunate, incurable desire, ending only with life, which it frequently shortens. I have been possessed with this desire from my childhood; it troubles me still now I am become older, and embitters many of my days. This insatiable curiosity to examine every thing myself, and foolish passion for adventures, has exposed me to many dangers, and been the occasion of much adversity and vexation: it has often rendered me unhappy, or forced me from the happiness I enjoyed.

I have already mentioned, that in order to escape from the English, with whom I was a prisoner of war, I had, at the imminent hazard of my life, ventured to sea in an open and leaky boat, in the middle of the tempestous monsoon. After a succession of unfortunate events, I at last arrived at Tranquebar. In my voyage from that place to the coast of Ceylon, I endured the greatest misery, and narrowly escaped with my life. This ought to have inspired me with an aversion to all dangerous undertakings, but, notwithstanding, my former passion soon revived; and, in a word, I wished to leave my enjoyments, the pleasant and happy life I led at Jaffnapatnam—Anna—all, for a time, and wander among the unexplored and savage forests of Ceylon. How imprudent soever such an inclination may appear to the reader, to expose myself among the wild beasts of the island, in order to examine them in the state of nature, I had often felt it since my arrival at Jaffnapatnam; but besides, there were in those immea-

of the water serpent, which unexpectedly seizes its long neck, and instantly bites it off with its sharp teeth. I have often seen such headless bodies of those birds floating on the water.

surable forests so many unknown plants, trees, insects, and thousands of things all peculiar to Ceylon, which I wished to see and examine, that I should willingly have penetrated even to *Condé-œda*, the metropolis of the emperor, to explore a country so famous in the ancient history of India, that I had heard so much of, and of which so few satisfactory accounts exist in Europe. There was not, however, the least probability that my wish would ever be gratified

To have ventured alone into those immeasurable forests which separate the Dutch possessions along the coast from those of the emperor of Condé œda, would have been foolish in the extreme; I should have lost myself even the first day, in those vast wildernesses, and must have been devoured by the monsters with which they are filled, or soon have perished with hunger.

The certainty that no European would be foolish enough to accompany me on such a journey, without an object, without knowledge, and without the hope of any great advantage, prevented me from speaking of it to any one, and made me consider it as an undertaking as unlikely to be accomplished as a voyage to the moon. I was, besides, unacquainted with any person capable of performing the journey, and with whom I could have ventured to expose myself to its dangers. My friend Templin was the only man in all Jaffnapatnam who, every thing considered, was best calculated for such an undertaking, he was strong, courageous, and hardened against fatigue; but the desire to learn any thing new, or curiosity after strange animals, plants, insects, &c. was not to be sought for in him. There was, therefore, not the least probability that he would expose himself for nothing and without reason, to hardships and dangers,—that he would leave his home, his wife and children, to undertake with me this unnecessary and perilous journey. Having once spoken of it to him, as if by chance, he only laughed, asking me if I was weary of my life; it was, however, no other than himself who, some time afterwards, invited me to the undertaking, of which I should otherwise have thought of no further.

One evening having gone to drink a glass of palm-wine and smoke a pipe with my neighbour, "You come quite a-propos," said he as soon as I entered the garden, "I was just going to send for you; having this morning received a letter with good news; my friend the overseer of the coopers, at *Colombo*, informs me that on account of bad health he has resolved to give up his charge, and return to Holland with the first ship: he has not yet made known his resolutions, but expects me within two months at Colombo to solicit the post vacant by his resignation, in which he and his friend will assist me with all their interest; here is the letter, read it yourself."

I congratulated the worthy *Templin* on his future prospects, and advised him not to delay, but to set out for *Colombo*, as early as possible, in a funny or other vessel, either in company or alone. " Do you take me for a fool," cried he, " what ! to fall into the hands of the English who are cruising along the whole coast of *Ceylon* and *Jaffnapatnam* and the straits of *Manar*—no, old *Templin* is not mad. I will go by land, and I have no doubt you will with pleasure accompany me on the journey." Though so fond of travelling this proposal did not exactly suit my taste. I told him that the road from *Jaffnapatnam* to *Colombo*, as many people had informed me, lay always close along the shore, and that nothing was to be met with by the way but poor villages, with miserable inhabitants, and that the whole journey could produce nothing to gratify my curiosity, or repay the expense of a *dooly* or *andol*,* as well as during my stay at *Colombo*, which altogether could not be less than a hundred rupees. " Besides which," said I, " you know that I am not alone, what should I do with *Anna*, it would not be advisable to leave her by herself."

" Give yourself no uneasiness with regard to *Anna*," replied he " she will stay with my wife till our return. Besides, it is by no means my intention to take the old common road along the shore, I should have no pleasure in that myself,—still less shall we be carried in an *andol* or *dooly*—we travel on foot," cried he clapping me on the shoulder,—" through the interior, high up in the country, across the great forest of *Ceylon*, which you have so often wished to do. You may now satisfy your curiosity while I shall indulge my inclination for the chase ; we shall go well armed with pistols, fowling-pieces, and cutlasses, and we must endeavour to find two or three *Europeans* or *Mestese*, willing to undertake the journey with us ; and besides each of us must hire a few Chivias† to carry our provisions and other necessaries ; and thus armed and prepared we shall have nothing to fear either from hunger or wild beasts."

It was unnecessary to say more, the wandering spirit rose in me like a smothered fire blown by the wind, and I joyfully gave him my hand, provided we could find two more Europeans to accompany us.

We talked over the subject for a considerable time, forming

---

* A sort of litter similar to a palanquin, except that the andol has a straight instead of a crooked bamboo, and no tent, but a piece of canvas several yards long, which hangs over it to exclude the sun's rays.

† The *chivias* belong to the lowest cast among the nations, and though they are not held in such contempt, by their countrymen, as the Parias among the natives of *Malabar* on the continent, yet they are kept in humble situations.

The *chivias* are not permitted to cover their heads with linen, or to ornament themselves with any thing of a black colour ; their wives and daughters must not cover the upper part of their bodies, but always go with their breasts bare. These chivias are used for the basest and lowest kind of labour.

new plans and decisions, till a message from *Anna* called me to supper, when, with my thoughts full of the journey, I returned to my habitation.

I said nothing of our intention that evening to *Anna*, knowing it would grieve her much; and that it would be time enough when the matter was more certain and brought to maturity; as all still depended upon the question, whether we could find in *Jaffnapatnam* two Europeans or Mestese, who, for our gratification alone, and without cause or necessity, would be willing to undertake so long and difficult a journey, even under the condition of being well paid for their trouble, and kept free of all expense. I looked upon this as an absolute impossibility, and therefore still placed little reliance on the journey's being accomplished. To venture myself alone in those frightful forests with my friend *Templin*, after mature deliberation, I concluded, would not be sufficiently prudent, and if merely any accident should happen to either of us, what course could the other pursue?

The affair therefore remained for some days in uncertainty, while Mr. *Templin*, in the interval, used every possible means to find among the free Europeans or Mestese, a couple of adventurers willing to accompany us in our intended journey. It was of no use to think of those in the company's service, as they were not at liberty to undertake such journeys, nor could they have left the garrison without running the risk of severe punishment.

At last, on the fourth day, my friend *Templin* informed me that he had found a third man, called *George*, who had formerly been a soldier at *Nagapatnam*, but was at that time out of the service.

I was not much pleased with this future fellow traveller. The man had two cardinal defects which, in my opinion, at once rendered him unfit for our undertaking, namely, he was deaf, and almost always drunk. In other respects he was a good fellow, always laughing and merry, notwithstanding his wretched condition, a great lover of every thing in the shape of strong liquor, unceasingly loquacious, and the most laughable and comic teller of a story that can possibly be imagined; for the rest, he was tall and strong, and by no means deficient in courage.

I knew him at Nagapatnam, where he had been a soldier in the company's service, and at the same time carried on the business of a baker. He was a native of Strasburgh, in which city he had also been a baker. A train of singular adventures and strange tricks, some of which I shall afterwards impart to the reader, were the cause of his being at *Jaffnapatnam*, where he contrived to exist through the generosity of some of the inhabitants. He had often expressed to us a wish to go to *Colombo*, to try the baking trade once more, at which he was certainly very expert, being at the same time an excellent and experienced cook; and had it not been for his unfortunate liking for liquor, he might have found a plentiful subsistence any where.

Although I was but little inclined towards him as a fellow traveller, I notwithstanding allowed myself to be persuaded by my friend *Templin*, who insisted that we were by no means obliged to give him more liquor than we should judge necessary; and for the rest, his deafness would not prevent him from assisting us if we were attacked by wild beasts.

I therefore gave my consent, and we sent for him. The proposals was no sooner made to accompany us, and that we would take him free of all expense to *Colombo*, than he joyfully agreed to it, and declared he was quite ready to set out. There were now three Europeans of us, but as we could not place too much dependence on our new comrade, it was absolutely necessary to increase our company by at least one more adventurer—Fortune favoured us in this beyond our expectation.

Some days after our last reinforcement, a person arrived at Jaffnapatnam, who called himself a Frenchman, but I afterwards discovered that he was a Swiss. He gave out that he was charged with important dispatches from admiral *De Suffren* to M. *Monneron*, the French agent, who was then at *Colombo*.

The dread of falling into the hands of the English, who were cruising round the island, and particularly in the straits of *Monar*, was also the reason of his wish to travel over land and on foot. His purse, probably, did not permit him to indulge himself with an andol. Not being willing to travel alone, he enquired among the inhabitants whether any European would in a short time set out on foot for *Colombo*. As our design was well known to the whole town, he was naturally directed to me; he came, and with much politeness requested me to permit him to join our party. I replied that I should rejoice to have him for my fellow traveller, but that I was afraid our manner of travelling would not be agreeable to him; it would therefore be necessary to make him acquainted with our plan before hand. We, it was true, were going to *Colombo*, but not by the usual road, which follows the line of the sea-shore: our intention was to get as far from it as possible, to take a south-easterly course to penetrate through the thick extensive forests, and over the mountains in the province of *Condé-œda* to the latitude of *Colombo*, towards which we should then take a westerly direction. We certainly had business to transact in that city, but we had undertaken the journey as much from curiosity and amusement, as from necessity; we therefore intended to travel at our ease, and without in the least hurrying ourselves, it being a matter of indifference whether we arrived a few weeks sooner or later at *Colombo*. If he could accommodate himself to this object and plan, and would promise not to interfere with them on the journey, but to identify himself entirely with us, my fellow travellers and myself would be happy to admit him into our party.

The route and our conditions were, however, far from giving him satisfaction, and he did his utmost to induce me to abandon our plan. He exposed in the most emphatic manner all the dangers and insurmountable difficulties with which we should have to struggle, in shaping a course for ourselves athwart impenetrable forests swarming with wild and savage beasts, where we might so easily lose ourselves, and be continually in danger of perishing, &c. But my new friend did not know me; all his eloquence was displayed in vain. Those dangers with which he endeavoured to frighten me from our intended journey, was one of the principal causes of my undertaking it. A journey without difficulties or dangers had few charms or attractions for me. All that is dreadful, beautiful, great or awful in nature, gave me pleasure—a hurricane, a tempestuous ocean, the roaring of thunder, the lightning shooting across the sky—I could behold with delight; the sight of abysses, precipices, mountains enveloped in clouds, sharp inaccessible overhanging cliffs, the rushing of cataracts, the falling of mountain streams into the echoing valley, and above all, thick and extensive forests full of grey massy trees and swarming with animals of every species, were so many enjoyments for my restless mind.

M. *D'Allemand* (so he called himself) at last finding that he could make no impression upon me, begged me to introduce him to my other fellow traveller. I immediately brought him to my friend *Templin*, who told him the same respecting the object of our journey that he had just heard from me. He used all the persuasion he was master of to induce Templin to give up the plan, by laying before him the dangers of the journey, but finding that here also he was preaching to the deaf, he at last declared himself ready to go with us, but begged at the same time that the preparations for the journey should be made with all possible dispatch. As we calculated the expense of provisions, drink, &c. for us and our chivias on the journey would amount together to 60 rupees, M. D'Allemand paid his 20 rupees without making any objections, and *Templin* took upon himself the charge of purchasing every thing necessary, which he thought would be ready within two days.

After we had arranged and regulated every thing respecting our arms, provisions, &c. we began the very next day to make preparations for our journey. I took three koolies or chivias into my service, my friend *Templin* as many, but as M. *D'Allemand* had a large trunk, he was obliged to take one more, so that our whole troop consisted of four Europeans and ten chivias or Indians, in all sixteen persons, including a slave belonging to M. D'Allemand and another to Mr. Templin. With respect to *George*, our baker, no assistance was necessary for him, as he carried his whole property upon his back, tied up in a bundle.

From the commencement of the war upon the coast, the annual hunting of the elephant had not taken place in Ceylon, as the merchants on the continent, who traded in those animals, did not come over to purchase them; and when, at last, the war broke out between the Dutch and the English, the former had enough to do to protect themselves from the attacks and stratagems of the latter, who frequently harassed them either by open violence, or by holding secret correspondence with the emperor, or sovereign of the island. The elephants had, therefore, become much bolder, and often leaving the forests and deep woods in large troops, occasioned great damage in the lonely and scattered villages; overturning the huts, and treading down the grain in the fields, or eating it up, and destroying many of the inhabitants. It was, therefore, highly necessary that we should be well armed, in order to protect ourselves from their attacks, and preserve our lives, or at least to possess some means of keeping them at a distance, or frightening them away, as a ball fired from a fowling-piece has but little effect upon their gigantic bodies. In consequence of this we provided ourselves with a hundred *fougeitos*,* or rockets, and two plates of copper to be used by way of cymbals, as those animals are most afraid of fire and loud noises, which they are unable to withstand in their wild state; but dependence cannot always be placed even upon this, as we in the sequel found by experience.

Having taken these precautions, I went to Mr. Raket, at that time governor of Jaffnapatnam, to request an *oppa* to Colombo, which I immediately received. The word *oppa* signifies an order, and serves the traveller for a passport.

There are two sorts of *oppas*,—those with white linen, and those without it. The first are given only to those who fill important offices, and to the Company's servants who are travelling on business to one or other of the Dutch Establishments in the island. Two days before the departure of the principal personage, a *Peon*, or courier, is sent out, who advertises all the villages at which the traveller is to stop, or pass through. The *Majorals*, or

* The Indians, in war, make use of a kind of rocket, which is called *fougeito*. It is an iron rod from 8 to 10 feet long, and about 8 inches thick. At the one end is a thick iron case filled with gun-powder, which, being fired by a small hole behind the case, the rod flies forward with amazing swiftness, turning continually round, and will sometimes kill or wound five or six men. These rockets are managed by particular persons, and both strength and art are necessary to let them off, and give them a horizontal direction.

heads of those villages, are expressly commanded, in such an *oppa*, to hang round the *ambalam** with white linen. The washer-women are required to provide this linen, being no other than the clothes which the villagers have sent to be washed. In this manner the gentleman's arrival is waited for; while, besides this, the Majoral, as well as his people, must supply him with provisions as long as he thinks proper to remain in the village. The heads of the villages are, by order of the Company, required to keep an accurate list of all the travellers who pass through their villages with such an *oppa*, and to deliver annually an account of all the expenses they are at, to the governor; but the money is seldom or never repaid to them.

The *oppa* without white linen is the leaf of a palm-tree, on which, in the *Malabar* or *Cingalese* language, every majoral is commanded to provide the bearer with what is necessary, upon his paying for it; such an *oppa*, which is refused to nobody, costs a rix-dollar. This precaution is absolutely necessary in a country where, from the oppression of their masters, the natives are exasperated to an extreme against all that are called Europeans, and, in consequence, never allow an opportunity to pass of injuring and molesting them to the utmost of their power.

CHAPTER III.

Anna's grief—Division of our baggage—Departure—Arrival at Calmonie—The Türmün—Conjugal history of the baker—Indisposition of Templin—Arrival at Panorin.

It was at last time to think of our departure:—all was ready, but I had the greatest difficulty in reconciling Anna to my departure, even in any degree. She was in despair as soon as she discovered my intention; her constant weeping and lamenting had almost made me change my resolution; while at the same time she endeavoured to persuade me that my undertaking was imprudent in the extreme, and that, though in a numerous company, I was not the less exposed to danger, and even to lose my life. This, however, as I have already said, was not a sufficient reason to deter me from undertaking the journey; but those sighs

* The *Ambelam* is a large square straw hut, which is found in every village, and serves the traveller instead of a *Chauderie*, (or kind of resting place,) which is not used in *Ceylon*.

and lamentations began, in some measure, to make me repent of having engaged myself so far in the business; and had it not been for shame, and the just reproaches of my other fellow travellers, who, relying upon my word and my company, had prepared every thing for the journey, I believe I should have, after all, withdrawn myself from the undertaking.

"A journey on foot," said Anna, "is ever pleasant and amusing, through inhabited and open countries, where people, habitations, villages, bazars, and halting places are found every where; but in those unbounded forests and wildernesses, where the deep silence that prevails is only interrupted by the hissing of serpents, or the howling of wild beasts: where no assistance or help of any kind can be looked for,—how easily may an accident befal you! The impenetrable high bushes through which you must struggle are the abode of venemous serpents and reptiles; and do you not also run great risk from the poisonous vapours of those deep woods, where a pure wind seldom blows, as well as from being overcome with fatigue or sickness, under which you might sink before you could be brought to an inhabited place."

I replied that it was now too late to think of retreating, but promised to take every possible care of my health, not to wander from the rest of the party, and to have a pair of boots made on purpose, that I might be less exposed to be bitten by serpents. As she saw the affair could not be altered, she became at last reconciled; and, on the day before our departure, took up her abode in the habitation of our friend *Templin*. The wife of the honest cooper had also in the beginning strongly opposed his entering into so dangerous an undertaking, and exposed the folly of making such an unnecessary journey, especially as he had a large family depending upon him for support. But the cooper had established the custom in his family, never to allow his wife to contradict or censure any of his measures. He would have proceeded in a plan, though perfectly convinced it was hurtful and disadvantageous, merely for the sake of contradicting her, if she had attempted to lay down rules for him, or blame his conduct. He was of a very selfish and obstinate temper, and she found it better to let him have his own way about the journey; reconciling herself as well as she could, and happy that she should at least enjoy the company of *Anna*.

On the morning of the day destined for our departure we all assembled in the cooper's house. Our first care was to divide the baggage and provisions among our people, and to appoint every one his share in the carriage.

Three chivias were set apart to carry the rice, the article of the first necessity; for this purpose we chose the strongest, and each of them was loaded with sixty pounds, which he carried over his shoulder upon a bamboo. Two others carried the trunk belonging to M. D'Allemand; the sixth had two large copper vessels, with narrow necks, called *Kodé*, each of which contained about a pailful of liquid; these vessels were destined for our supply of fresh water. The seventh kooly carried two baskets, in which were our liquors, coffee, tea, sugar, and the cocoa-oil and spices for the curry; he was besides loaded with twenty-five pounds of rice. The eighth was charged with the furniture of the kitchen, consisting of two large copper pots to boil rice, besides several copper scales, instead of plates, and four jugs of the same metal to drink out of; he also had twenty-five pounds of rice. Our hundred *Fougeitos*, or rockets, and the mats to eat and sleep upon, with a pair of small round cushions for our heads, formed the burden of the ninth. The clothes and linen of my friend *Templin*, and my own, (we had provided ourselves only with what was absolutely necessary) were, with some trifling articles, carried by the tenth man. M. D'Allemand's slave-boy was our cymbal player, or rather beater, and carried at the same time a leather bag with our ammunition, powder, balls, and cartridges; while the cooper's boy was to beat upon the other cymbal, and act as cook upon the journey.

All being now prepared, we partook of a hasty dinner with the cooper in his garden, and after taking a tender farewell of the females, who could not refrain from melting into tears, the whole train set forward, with cymbals playing, and accompanied by a great number of the inhabitants, who had come to see this singular cavalcade.

The four Europeans bore a considerable resemblance to a troop of freebooters going out upon an expedition. *Templin*, M. *D'Allemand*, and myself, had each a hanger at his side, a pair of pistols in his girdle, a cartridge-box before him, and a musket upon his shoulder; and the deaf baker was armed with a long hussar sabre, which struck upon the ground at every step he took.

It was three o'clock in the afternoon when we set out, and at four we arrived at *Colomgamme*, otherwise called *Colombatoor*, a small fishing village situated on the gulf of *Catchaï*. The boats for the conveyance of travellers across the bay, are stationed at this place; each person pays two stivers, (about two-pence,) for his passage.

Mr. *Schröter*, secretary of the police, who was present at our departure, had arrived before us, in his palanquin,* at this place, and given orders to have three boats in readiness. We imme-

* A litter made of bamboo, which is carried by koolies or bearers, and is very secure and convenient for travelling, as the occupier may sleep, sit, read, and even write in it.

diately embarked our chivias and baggage in two of them, while we, with Mr. Schröter and some friends who had accompanied us thus far, emptied a few more bottles of wine, which they had brought with them.

At last, about five o'clock, we took leave of our friends, and embarked for the other side.

The wind was directly against us, so that the sails were of no use, and we were obliged to row. On the passage, a *türmün*, or arrow-fish, shot over the vessel, and so close to our baker's face, that the fright made him let fall a glass of wine which he had just put to his mouth to drink success to our journey.

The word *türmün* signifies, as has been already said, arrow-fish; and it is not without reason that this name has been given it;—an arrow from a bow does not cleave the air so rapidly as this fish when it rises out of the water to escape the pursuit of its enemy. It is commonly about two feet in length; in shape and colour it greatly resembles the pike, but is somewhat thinner; its snout is like the beak of a bird, amazingly hard, tapering to a point, and projects at least half a foot from its head. It is frequently caught on account of its delicate flavour, but it is not very abundant. It shoots, in an instant, upwards of twenty paces through the air in a right line, and sometimes pierces the deck of a vessel with its long pointed snout, which is with great difficulty extricated, and it is often necessary to break it off. The fishermen of this bay, who, according to custom, have commonly the one half of their bodies under water, either to drive the fish into their nets, by beating the water with a stick, or to catch tortoises, are much afraid of the türmüns, and are often exposed to be wounded by them. There are many instances of people having been struck by them, and lost their lives, and this might unfortunately have been the fate of our poor baker, if the fish had struck him in the temples, above which it was little more than a span when it shot past him; he certainly would not have lived to tell the tale.—To what singular deaths are men sometimes exposed!

In my walks along the bay of *Catchaï*, I have often seen this fish shoot out of the water, and have always remarked in it a visible singular thrilling motion, when it flew along the surface of the water; and no doubt it is this general shuddering or trembling of its body which carries it for a few moments into the air, and gives this amazing power and rapidity to its motion.

We landed about six o'clock on the other side of the gulf, which is *Ceylon*, properly so called. Our people, who, as I have said, set out an hour before us, had taken up their quarters under a large *bangalo*, situated not far from the beech, and apparently serving as a shelter from the sun and the rain, for passengers and their goods, waiting the arrival of a vessel from *Colombogamme*, to carry them over to the peninsula of *Jaffnapatnam*.

We were overjoyed that they had chosen this place instead of the fishing village *Calmonia*, about a hundred yards from it, where we should have been obliged to pass the night either in or among the fishers' huts. When we arrived, our cook and the chivias had the rice-pot already on the fire, and our supper was soon prepared. We ordered the mats to be spread under a large thickly-leafed tree that stood before the bangalo. Here we supped; and afterwards prepared ourselves to sleep in the same place. But the baker, who had paid too many visits to our bottle, put sleep out of the question with his continual babbling, nor could all our remonstrances prevail on him to be quiet.

At last, recollecting the tender farewell that Anna and I took of each other at our departure, and the tears she shed on that occasion,—"Truly, sir," said he, turning towards me with a satirical grin, "if you knew the women as well as I do, if they had plagued, beaten, banished, and ruined you, as they have me, you would not make so much ado about them, and still less would you put any trust in their crocodile tears. As I am in a talking humour," continued he, "and have not the least inclination to sleep, I must, to pass away the time, give you some account of my life, in so far as the fair sex are concerned, and all the miseries and misfortunes they have brought upon me. Alas! they are the cause that I am now compelled to wander about like a vagabond, and to lead a poor, miserable, and wretched life. You shall judge whether I have not good reason to curse and detest that false, treacherous, inconstant, and faithless sex."

After this introduction he began an account of his life, which was every moment interrupted by imprecations, and the abuse of women. As he spoke with the Strasburgh accent, a mixed dialect of bad Dutch and German, thickly interspersed with oaths, and at the same time accompanied the relation of his adventures with ridiculous gestures, and a distorted countenance, it was impossible for us to forbear from now and then bursting out into a loud laugh.

He had married four wives in different cities in Europe, who, as far as he knew, when he went to India, were all living, and unknown to one another. They had caused him all the evils that ever base and wicked women can possibly bring upon a man. His domestic history, which he related at full length, was truly strange and humorous.

He was forced to leave his first wife, for fear of his life; she was a devil in human shape. The second had sold him to a Prussian recruiting party, and he had the misfortune to lose his hearing at the battle of *Rosbach*. The third, who was a spendthrift and tippler, soon reduced him from the comfortable situation he was in when he had the misfortune to marry her, to a state of beggary. The fourth, whom he espoused at Hamburg, betrayed him into the hands of the Dutch *Zielverkoopers*,* or *kidnappers*, and was sent by them as a soldier to *Nagapatnam*. He began the baking trade there, and would have succeeded extremely well, had it not been for his continual tippling, to which he had, like many others, become addicted from endeavouring to stifle the feelings of domestic misery. He there married his fifth wife, a black Paria girl of the Roman Catholic religion; she was young, and her exterior appearance was not at all unfavourable. She served, as maid, a European soldier's wife called *Barbara*, who kept a coffee-shop. Our baker saw her, and through the persuasion of Barbara, he was so extremely imprudent as to marry her.

Some days afterwards I happened by chance to pass his house with some friends; we entered to see how he and his young wife were succeeding; but what was our surprise to find the house open, and completely empty; no people, no furniture, no baking materials; nothing was to be seen. We then went to Barbara, who lived in the neighbourhood, to enquire if *George* had removed. She told us that he had been taken the day before to the hospital, where he was lying very ill; of his wife she knew nothing. Curiosity induced me, some time after, to go to the hospital to see him. I there found him in a state which excited my commiseration, suffering the most dreadful agonies, having taken an antidote to expel the poison which his fifth wife had made him a present of.

Such was the history of our *George*, abridged. My companions had fallen asleep in the middle of his long-winded story; but as I had no inclination to sleep, and indeed did not consider it worth while, as the day would soon dawn, I lighted a segar, and wandered along the adjacent shore of the bay.

The heavens were still in all their splendour, sown with glittering stars, and the queen of night, unobscured by vapours spread upon the water, the sandy downs, and the trees, a soft and melancholy light. The gentle, but unceasing ripple of the light waves, which broke upon the shore, the silence, the solitude which prevailed around me, awoke in my soul an irresistible train of melancholy ideas.

I sat down at the foot of a tree, and after having, for some time, contemplated the image of the moon, which danced upon the moving water, I gave myself up to my reflections. I recalled to my mind the narrative of George the baker, and could not avoid concluding that in all he had suffered it was

* Soul-sellers.—Trans.

fortunate that his want of feeling had freed him from all anguish to which they are exposed who possess susceptible affections.

He had never loved, he knew not what love was; the pangs of tormenting jealousy had never torn his heart; he had married his wives either from persuasion, or because he considered a creature of that kind to be necessary in his house, and he had left them all without the least regret.

That sensibility and tenderness of soul that is so highly prized, but which is, in reality, one of the most fatal gifts that man can receive from nature, was altogether unknown to him. Would to God that I had been endowed with as small a portion of it, how many miseries, how many distresses and misfortunes, how much anguish of soul should I have escaped.

I was awoke from my meditations by a noise and movement at our resting place. The stars had began to appear dim in the east, the confused noise of the crows, which were leaving, in troops, the trees which had served them for a shelter during the night; the rustling and chirping of whole droves and swarms of birds of all sorts, preparing to salute the dawn with their songs and voices, announced the approaching day.

I returned to our halting place, where I found our chivias occupied with the rice and cany,* which was left the evening before. While some were busy in making fast our luggage to sticks or bamboos, at the end of which they carried it, and after a slight breakfast, we re-commenced our journey. We left the common road that passes by the village of *Paniacoor*, in order to avoid the deep sand, and followed the shores of the gulf of *Catchai*.

The sun now rose in full majesty: the heaven was blue and clear, and the scarcely-opened dawn gave to all the objects around me a youthful and enchanting appearance; the finely-bending shores of the gulf, bordered with high trees, the overhanging branches of which were reflected on the blue surface of the water; the gentle breath of the cool morning wind; the monotonous plashing of the light waves; the screaming of the sea-gulls, that skimmed in circles, the surface of the water; the melodious pipe of the red-legged snipes, calling to each other; the innumerable water-fowl, rising from the thick groves of reeds, produced in me the most delightful sensations, and, at that moment, all the dangers, all the difficulties, of our intended journey were forgotten.

We had been scarcely a quarter of an hour on the way, when our baker, after having turned all his pockets inside out, suddenly

* Rice-water.

uttered a most lamentable howl, and begged us not to leave him behind while he ran back to our last night's resting place in search of two rupees, the only two he had in the world, which he must have lost there.

All that we could say to persuade him from taking this unnecessary trouble was in vain, he seemed determined to return; we were therefore obliged to give him two rupees in place of those he had lost, that we might not be prevented from proceeding on our journey.

After having followed the course of the shore upwards of a mile, we left the sea and struck right into the country; and after walking two hours among sand hills, some of which were covered with palm-trees, we arrived at an *ambelan*, or halting place, erected at the entrance of a village called *Manoor*, situated in the middle of the sand hills.

Let it not, however, be supposed that such resting places are like the *chandries*, on the coast of Bengal, &c. among which are generally to be found convenient, and often large, handsome, and even splendid buildings. No—the halting places that we meet with, which was not very often in the whole of our journey, were almost all huts covered with straw, and so small that they could not contain ten men; and this is always the case in every part of the island. Travellers in Ceylon are but poorly accommodated with night quarters, and commonly pass the night under a tree, or, if it is in the rainy reason, under their *Talpat*.*

The *chanderies*, as well as many other benevolent institutions, which are spread in so great number, from the utmost bounds of Hindostan to the farthest frontiers of Malabar, are alone sufficient to prove that the old inhabitants of those countries were a very different people from those of the island of Ceylon, as well in religion and morals, as in opinions, and in every respect quite a distinct race. Such piety and benevolence, and dispositions so gentle, were certainly not to be found among the last-

* This tree is called talpat by the Indians, and derives its name from two Malabar words, talay and pat, that is, head and leaf, or headleaf, because these leaves are used by the natives to protect them from the sun and rain. They are about a yard and a half in diameter, and of a circular form. Being folded like a fan, they are carried upon the head, with the point turned forward; only the principal people in the kingdom of Candy have the privilege of carrying them with the broad part before. In Malabar, only people who are of a very high *cast*, or who fill important offices, are permitted to have a slave to carry the talpat behind them. The Portuguese and Mestese ladies are so fond of this luxury, that they never go out, even in the finest weather, without a slave to attend them with a parasol of this kind.

The tree, on the top of which these leaves grow, is uncommonly straight and tall. It produces only in the last stage of existence, a fruit about the size of a nut, but unfit to be eaten, and serving only to continue the species: the leaves which fall from it have a strong and unpleasant smell.

mentioned people, and it might easily be shown, that this Island was formerly inhabited by a wild and savage nation, who lived by invading and plundering the continent. They are mentioned in the ancient Indian histories under the fictitious name of giants, who were at last attacked and completely destroyed by *Ramed*. But to return to our journey. After our chivias had rested a little, and drank the callow or palm-wine, we set out once more, through a barren sandy district, full of downs, most of which were covered with palm-trees, and some with cocoa-trees to the top. We saw no villages, except a few scattered and solitary huts. This district seemed to be but little cultivated, and was very poorly provided with food for the inhabitants.

It was now about eleven o'clock, and we could discern at a distance, across an extensive sandy plain, the fort of *Panorin*; when the *cooper*, who had complained of a severe colic after our departure from *Manoor*, suddenly threw himself down at the foot of a tree, which overhung a small hut, and declared he could proceed no further. As he began to consider his life near an end, he requested us to send one of his people back to *Jaffnapatnam*, with all possible haste, to bring an andol that he might be conveyed home to his family.

We endeavoured to convince him that the andol could not be brought till late in the evening of the next day, and that within that time he would either recover or be carried off by the disease; and instead of sending any body to *Jaffnapatnam*, we used all the means in our power to assist him.—Rubbing arrack, all that we could think of was tried and expected to give him relief, but in vain,—the pain increased to such a degree that I actually began to entertain little hope of his recovery.

While we were thus occupied, and quite at a loss what further remedies to apply, a reverend old man came out of the hut before which our patient lay, and asked us what our comrade complained of. We informed him what it was, and at the same time our suspicion that he had brought the disorder upon him at *Manoor*, by drinking lunyas, or the water of unripe cocoa-nuts, while he was heated with walking, which, as we supposed, had occasioned a sudden chillness in his stomach.

The old man immediately went into the hut and returned with something tied up in a betel-leaf, which he gave our fellow traveller to chew, telling him at the same time to swallow the juice of it. This remedy had the desired effect, and gave him so much relief that in half an hour he found himself able to recommence the journey. We therefore set out once more after thanking the old man for his assistance, and the cooper had offered him a couple of rupees, but which he stedfastly refused to accept.

With slow steps we approached Panorin, over the sandy plain

which separated us from it. The sun scorched us excessively; his rays had heated to an extreme, and it was already two o'clock when we arrived at the fort.

The commandant of this fort received us in the most friendly manner; his name was *Koning*, and he was, as he told us, seventy-five years old. I have never seen in India a European of so great an age and at the same time of so fresh and healthy an appearance; nobody could have supposed that he was more than fifty years old. He had been stationed at the post of *Panorin* for thirty years. No sooner had he heard of our comrade *Templin's* illness than he presented him with a large glass of an infusion of the colomba root, which at once freed him from his colic. He had, in the mean time, caused dinner to be prepared, and invited us to partake of a wild boar he had shot the day before: hunting he told us had always been his chief and most agreeable amusement in this lonely and remote situation. There were in his face, and in different parts of his body, several large and deep scars, left by wounds he had received from a tiger. The beast had fallen upon him unawares, and thrown him down with the spring he made at him: in the struggle that took place, he fortunately had time to draw out a knife which he carried in his girdle, and with it rip open the belly of the monster, at the moment he was ready to become its prey. He showed us the hide, which he still kept as a token of his bravery and good fortune.

Panorin is situated under the government of *Jaffnapatnam*. The company have stationed here a serjeant and twelve soldiers, all invalids, with some Lascars, or Native soldiers, the same as those called Cipais upon the coast. The fort, built by the Portuguese, the former possessors of Ceylon, is of a square form, and miserably small; it has only two bastions on two opposite corners, and is now almost untenable, being little better than a heap of stones. The village lies to the south of the fort, and has also not the most flourishing appearance, consisting only of about a hundred miserable huts, from which may easily be inferred the poverty of the inhabitants. The district round *Panorin* is, with this exception, very thinly inhabited, sandy, and barren, owing to the bad quality of the water, which is very brackish and unwholesome.

Koning, the serjeant or commander at *Panorin*, made great complaints against the wild elephants; they had some days before overturned and completely destroyed a magazine of *neli*, or rice, belonging to him. They came in whole troops in the most furious manner from the woods, and caused great damage to the inhabitants; and they were so bold that neither fires nor noises could frighten them. He was of opinion that a general hunting expedition should be undertaken against them, in order to drive them back into the deep recesses of the forests, and he advised, and even begged us to give up our intention of penetrating into the country, laying before us, in the strongest point of view, the danger we should incur. The cooper and I, however, could not be persuaded to relinquish our design ; but M. *D'Allemand*, terrified by the serjeant's representatians of the danger, did all in his power to induce us to give it up.

As soon as we had dined, preparations were made for our departure ; we loaded our pistols and musquets with ball, put new flints in the locks, and after taking a hearty farewell of our friendly serjeant, we set out altogether upon our expedition.

It might now be about four o'clock: we left the common road, which runs southward, and made directly for the woods, which lay about half a mile to the east of us, occupying a vast extent of the horizon. It was a noble and magnificent prospect to see before us such a dark and immeasurable forest, the abode of innumerable multitudes of savage, wild, carnivorous, and gigantic animals, of every size and description ; and I must confess that I was not altogether free of fear and uneasiness as we continued to approach it. An involuntary feeling of astonishment and awe struck me when we entered its dark shades, as we had already observed recent marks of the elephants in passing over the sandy plain which separates *Panorin* from the borders of the forest.

CHAPTER IV.

Dreadful rencontre with a bear—Shoumberongonde—Negligence —Polverencadoo—The Forest at night—The Apes—The Bonkedoor.

WE now entered those dark and awful shades, and continued our journey between the high majestic columns that supported the green vault intermingled with flowers over our heads ; a soft melancholy feeling encircled us, which increased as we continued to advance.

The forest was at first open and free, and the trees were tall and straight, though they did not appear to be very old ; but as we proceeded they became larger, and stood much closer together. Underwood and brambles sometimes connected whole groves so closely, that we frequently could not proceed ten paces without cutting our way with a hatchet ; and we were extremely glad when our guide brought us to a narrow serpentine footpath, in which we were to follow through the forest.

This guide was one of our chivias, or koolies, a man who had formerly been a vaidana, or elephant-hunter, and had traversed the forests of Ceylon by night as well as by day. He spoke the Cingalese language, and had even been at Candé-Udda, and among the *Vaddahs** and it was from his informatian that I collected many particulars respecting these people. We were overjoyed at finding this man, and we paid him double what the other koolies received, but, as will be seen afterwards, he was not so useful to us as we had expected.

The path we now followed, which, as near as I could judge, had a south-east direction, was so uncommonly narrow, that only one person had sufficient room to walk in it. Paths of this kind run here and there through those thick woods, and some traverse the whole island; there are three or four which lead to Candé-Udda, and the interior of the country. It is a most singular circumstance, that they are all bordered on both sides with a hedge double the height of a man, which are so steep and perpendicular, and so close and even on the outside, that they might be supposed to have been planted by the hand of man, and clipped and kept smooth by an experienced gardener.

We had scarcely followed this path a quarter of an hour when I met with an adventure, which had almost put an end to my life and journey together.

The path, as I have already said, was extremely narrow; we were, therefore, obliged to walk one behind another, like a flock of wild geese. M. D'Allemand and I were at the head of the troop; we were walking next one another, and deeply engaged in conversation, when, all of a sudden, a bear of uncommon size rushed out of the hedge directly before us, apparently with the design of crossing the path. The closeness of the hedge had, no doubt, prevented him from seeing us, and the quickness of his motion from scenting us at a distance.

The unexpected appearance of this monster, which stood di-

---

* The most singular part of the inhabitants of Ceylon are the *Vuddahs*, or *Bedahs*, who inhabit the distant recesses of the forests. Their origin has never been traced, and they appear to differ very much from the other inhabitants of Ceylon. They are scattered over the woods in different parts of the island, but are most numerous in the province' of Bintan, which lies to the north-east of Candy, in the direction of Trincomalee and Batacole, and are there more completely in the savage state than any where else. They subsist by hunting deer, and other animals of the forest, and on the fruits which grow spontaneously around them; but they never cultivate the ground in any manner. They sleep on trees, or at the foot of them, and climb up like monkeys when alarmed. A few of the less wild traffic with the natives, giving ivory, honey, wax, and deer, in exchange for cloth, iron, and knives: but the wilder class, known by the name of Rambah Vedahs, are more seldom seen, even by stealth, than the most timid of the wild animals. The dogs of the Vedahs constitute their only riches, and are described as possessing wonderful sagacity.

W. Read Sc.

Rencontre with a Bear.

rectly before me, and, apparently, undecided whether to attack me, or turn back, prevented me from retreating, and so suddenly did this take place, that before I was aware, I had tumbled over his broad back, and fallen to the ground on the other side. As the path was here too narrow for two of us to go abreast, we marched in a sort of oblique manner; M. D'Allemand being therefore a pace behind me when the bear made his appearance, had time to save himself.

In the mean while I had, as soon as I fell, instantly endeavoured to get up again, in order to escape, or defend myself, but there was no time for this; I saw the bear standing near me with his paws lifted up, growling and ready to fall upon me. I had scarcely raised myself half up when this dreadful sight made me fall back, and rendered it impossible for me to save myself. All human assistance seemed to be unavailing, as the smallest movement, either of myself or my companions, would have made the bear strike his claws into my head, above which they were suspended. He appeared only to be collecting his strength in order to be sure of his aim. I gave up my soul to God, and waited for death with closed eyes. At this decisive moment I heard something whistle past my ears, and at the same time a report took place, which frightened the bear to such a degree that, instead of attacking me, he raised a frightful howl, and fled through the same opening in the forest by which he had come.

I have seldom been so near the end of my life, not only from the bear, that, by a single stroke of his paws, in which they possess incredible strength, could have split my head, but much more from the ball, which M. D'Allemand had, with a trembling hand, fired at him, and which I heard whistle close to my head. It was, however, this pistol shot that saved my life; because, though my fellow-travellers and the koolies, who were some paces behind, had instantly come to my relief, it would only have hastened the moment of my destruction. It was also fortunate that the shot did not strike the bear, as in that event he would have torn me in pieces either in his agony or fall.

While my fellow-travellers were congratulating me on my escape, the baker was endeavouring to creep through the hedge, in order, with his sword, to attack the bear, which he believed to be still in the neighbourhood. After several fruitlesss attempts, finding that it was impossible to penetrate the hedge, on account of the thorns, he declared he would, at least, show us an infallible method of putting the most savage and boldest animals to flight. For this purpose he put his hat between his teeth, began to crawl upon his hands and feet, and to howl and roar in such a manner, accompanied with such singular and surprising leaps, that we could not forbear laughing; and his drollery had at least the effect of restoring us all to good humour.

As the path wound in a serpentine direction through the wood, which prevented our seeing to any great distance before us, it was possible that other accidents of the same sort might befal us. If an elephant, or other wild animal, had happened to come in the opposite direction, it would have been impossible to get out of its way in time to save ourselves, the road being so extremely crooked as well as narrow. In order to avoid such accidents in future, as much as possible, we resolved to place our cymbal players, and two of our koolies, armed with pikes, twenty paces in advance of our caravan, who were to give the alarm upon the first appearance of danger. After this we marched forward with more confidence and security.

The evening now began to fall, and the thickness of the forest increased the darkness. The wild beasts were heard now and then at a distance, and we were still far from the place where our guide proposed that we should spend the night. We therefore lighted the torches that the serjeant at Panorin had made us a present of, as we durst not proceed any further in the dark. These torches are branches of a very resinous wood that burns as clear as a flambeau. The whole forest was illuminated by them to a considerable distance, which formed a very grand spectacle. The sharp clang of the cymbals awoke all the feathered inhabitants of the woods, and being dazzled by the strong light, they flew around us in confused multitudes. Many apes also, disturbed in their rest on branches of the trees, expressed their dissatisfaction by throwing fruit and pieces of wood at us.

At last, about nine o'clock, we arrived, worn out with fatigue, at a solitary ambellan in the midst of the forest, that had more the appearance of a ruinous hut than a resting place. We resolved to pass the night under the open heaven, as the straw roofs of such places are often the abode of serpents. We then kindled a large fire, before which we were to sleep, and three more on the opposite sides, at some paces distant from us, as there was no want of dry wood. Our supper consisted of a piece of wild boar, of which the hospitable fort-keeper at *Panorin* had supplied us with a tolerable provision for our journey. In order to prevent the fires from going out, and to secure us from the attacks of wild beasts during the night, we had agreed that one of us, with two of our koolies, should keep watch, which was to be relieved by the same number every two hours. After having taken these precautions, we lay down and passed the night in tranquillity; and though we heard the roaring of tigers, and many other voices unknown to us, we were not disturbed by them.

The next morning we left this place, which was called *Shoum-*

Berongonde. Our passage became more difficult as we advanced; the path was often lost among the brambles, or obstructed by the branches which the elephants had torn from the trees to feed upon the leaves, and, sometimes, for whole hours together, the hedge which had formerly bordered the path, was so low, that we could not distinguish it from the underwood among which it grew. This afforded us an opportunity of examining the forest more closely; we found abundance of trees and plants, many of which were unknown to me, and had never met with on the Continent.

How lovely, how inexpressibly delightful is the early dawn of morning in those woods. All is full of life, every part teems with existence. Apes with their young ones, skipping from one branch to another, with the most singular gestures and grimaces; birds of the most magnificent plumage, sailing through the air; flocks of peacocks, which adorn the lofty groves, spreading all their splendour and beauty to the sun's rays, piercing through the green foliage. The most delicious and invigorating air is inhaled from the odoriferous plants that bloom unseen among the underwood; a refreshing coolness surrounds you; the confused noise and chirping of millions of birds, the monotonous hum of the insects that swarm around you;—all fills the soul with an unspeakable tranquillity and enjoyment, which can be felt no where else but in the forests of India.

A fatal accident had nearly happened to us at thisplace.

Before we set out I had lighted a cegar by means of a tinder-box. After shutting it properly as I supposed, I returned it into a bag that the cooper's slave-boy carried, and in which a great part of our gunpowder, and about sixty musquet and pistol cartridges were. But what was our amazement and terror when, not long after, having occasion to take something out of the bag, we discovered that the tinder-box, not having been properly shut, the burning tinder had fallen out of it, and had already set fire to one of the cartridge papers, and after consuming one side of it almost to the powder, had gone out of itself. What a dreadful event might have taken place. The poor slave boy, as well as every one near him at the moment of the explosion, would undoubtedly have been the victims of one of the most lamentable and fatal of misfortunes. This terrible fate must have been mine, as I always made the boy walk by my side that the tinder-box might be always at hand for my cegars. It will be readily concluded that we placed it no more in the ammunition bag.

For the first time we saw among the trees a herd of wild boars and swine, with their young ones, which rushed through the wood at full gallop, not far from us, but without taking the least notice of us, at which we were heartily glad, as they are very mischievous and dangerous animals when they have young ones, and are approached too near. We saw here and there small groups of deer, some of which, thinking themselves too near us, set off at full speed, while others more confident from their distance, contented themselves with standing immovable and gazing at us. Hares were in such abundance that M. *D'Allemand* and the cooper shot four without going out of the path.

About eleven o'clock in the forenoon we came to a straw hut, called *polvcrencadoo.* A little farther on we found a well with clear fresh water, which happened very opportunely for filling our kodas, or water-pitchers, they being now almost empty. It was in fact a glorious discovery for us, as there is commonly a want of fresh water, in this part of the island where the ground is flat and sandy, in the dry season: what is then found in pools and holes is for the most part brackish and dirty.

We made here an excellent dinner of the hares we had shot, which we found much more tender and delicate than the peacocks, the flesh of which, though uncommonly white, is hard and dry. I therefore advised the cooper not to shoot any more of those beautiful birds, especially as the woods abounded with all sorts of game.

While we are at dinner I shall give the reader an account of the manner in which we passed the nights in our progress through the forest.

The places where water was to be found in the neighbourhood had always the preference, and we laid ourselves down on any spot where the ground appeared to be cleanest and least covered with underwood.

The ground was no sooner chosen and marked out than we spread upon the sand our mats, which served us for tables, chairs, and bed. Some of the koolies ran in search of dry wood and leaves in order to make a fire; after which our meal was got ready and those among us who were the most fatigued, lay down in the interval to sleep. Some sang, others smoked, or walked about till the repast was prepared; when assembled in small groups of three or four, beneath a large tree, with their legs crossed under them, and each with his plate of leaves before him, they finished their meal. A little further, we sat with our venison, or curry, before us, on plates of the same sort. Mirth, jesting, and laughter, prevailed at our repast, for which the drollery of the baker supplied us with abundance of occasions. No sooner was it finished, than the plates were all thrown away, the pots and pans were cleaned, and every thing again packed up; after which we lay down to sleep for two hours. The time being expired, those who had the watch called us up, and instantly all were in motion. The baggage was made fast, the koolies resumed their burdens, and we re-commenced our journey with fresh courage.

But when we came to our halting-place, towards night, we were more particular in our choice of it, and used a great many more precautions. We now carefully avoided those places where water was to be found, that we might not be disturbed by the wild beasts which then leave their dens in search of prey, and usually, before setting out, quench their thirst, or wash themselves in the marshes or pools. We sought particularly a spot of ground free from underwood and brambles, and where the wood was in some measure open and free.

One of us, with a loaded pistol in each hand, and the baker, with his naked sword, accompanied the koolies, who went in search of dry wood, of which we required a considerable quantity, not only for the great fire round which we lay, but also for several smaller ones which we were obliged to kindle round us for our security.

Our meal was now prepared, and eaten much more quietly than during the day. We were less lively and cheerful; this was occasioned by fatigue, as well as by a certain restless melancholy, which I cannot easily describe. There is always something in darkness that fills the soul with awe, and deprives it of cheerfulness; we crept close to each other, and every one was afraid to remove from the fire. As those woods are delightful during the day, so are they terrifying and awful in the night.

It is no longer the same extended forest which, the same morning, resounded with the cheerful and intermingled notes of birds. The beautiful yellow light spread over the wood by the sun's rays through the thick foliage, has given place to thick darkness; a death-like silence prevails instead of the loud song with which the feathered inhabitants of the wood greeted the dawn of the now expired day. Only the sorrowful hooting of the night-owl is heard at intervals, which, repeated by a melancholy echo, fills the soul with terror:—then the howling and intermingled roar of jackals, tigers, and other wild beasts, heard at a distance, is suddenly succeeded by a stillness like that of the grave. From another quarter is heard the cracking of branches and young trees, which the elephants are breaking and tearing up, to feed upon the leaves. All at once a dreadful trampling approaches, and a noise, and cracking, as if half a city were in flames; it seems as if a hurricane were rushing through the tops of the trees, the ground trembles as when shaken by an earthquake, and a confused sound, like that of a multitude of trumpets, seems to be the signal for an attack. In a word, it is a troop of some hundreds of the largest elephants, who, after having consumed all the food round their former haunt, are emigrating to some other part of the forest, making their way through the wood by main force, cutting out a course by overthrowing and trampling down all that comes in their way, except trees of a great height and thickness. It is impossible for me to convey any thing like an idea of the noise and cracking occasioned by the breaking and splitting of so many hundreds of trees. Some conception of it, however, may be formed, by recollecting the crash occasioned by a single tree of moderate size, when broken in the middle of the stem like a reed; and it may easily be calculated how small this is, compared with the multitude of trees in so wide a compass as was necessary to allow a passage to so many elephants, and those all broken at the same time. Add to this the trembling of the earth, occasioned by the trampling of so many of those animals, one of which shakes the ground on which he walks. All this, accompanied by a loud confused sound, like that of trumpets, and some faint idea may be formed of this indescribable and terrific noise. Alas! I little imagined that I should soon be placed in a situation where I should have but too much time to make myself familiar with such, and still more terrifying objects. But of this in its proper place.

After having finished our dinner at *Polverencadoo*, we set out about three o'clock in the afternoon, and a short time after came to the entire carcase of an elephant, which lay near the path. The animal must have been long dead; it had, however, beautiful teeth, of uncommon length and thickness. Our way became very difficult here; the path was obstructed every moment by fallen and decayed trees, and we had often the greatest possible difficulty to trace it among the brambles, and open for ourselves a passage through the thickets and bushes with which it was overgrown. In this manner we continued our journey with much difficulty, till we came, about five o'clock, to a brook of clear fresh water, through which we waded. When we had proceeded on the other side for some time, we remarked that the wood became more open, and less obstructed by bushes. The path, which for a long time past had ceased to be bordered by a hedge, was here entirely lost, and we were obliged to trust ourselves to the direction of a small map which I had with me. We took a south-west course.

Here we fell in with a troop of deer, which gazed at us with outstretched necks, in fixed amazement. Their attention was so completely fastened upon us, that the cooper had time to shoot one of them. The report had no sooner taken place, than we instantly heard something not far from us, fall to the ground. The bear, (for it was one,) had, as soon as he reached earth, took to flight, growling at us, and we soon lost sight of him. Our guide supposed that he had ascended the tree to rob the bees of their honey. We approached the tree, and saw a swarm of bees flying about in it, but from the thickness of the leaves, and the darkness which already began to fall, we could discover nothing more. The cooper and the baker skinned the deer, and having kept the best pieces of it, we left the remainder, and proceeded on our way. By this and similar incidents we had lost much time, and the day drew to a close. A dim twilight already began to spread through the wood, and we could scarcely discern objects at a moderate distance from us. The birds had retired to their resting places, for it no sooner begins to grow dark, than the plumed songsters cease their music, and hide themselves among the thick foliage. After having provided ourselves plentifully with water, we took up our quarters at some distance from the brook we had passed over, that we might not disturb the wild beasts which resorted to it, in order to quench their thirst.

Notwithstanding, however, all our endeavours not to molest the original inhabitants of the woods, we found it impossible to avoid it altogether.

The unusual noise and tumult occasioned by so many people, and the cutting of dry branches and bushes, which we found necessary to be done daily, having observed recent marks of elephants and buffaloes on this as well as the other side of the brook, together with the cracking of the flame, which illuminated the wood to a distance around us,—had occasioned terror and confusion among a colony of apes, which seemed exclusively to inhabit this part of the forest, and before our arrival had slept in the trees in peace. The first that awoke were those directly above us and our fire, and they immediately, by their dismal yells, spread terror among their more distant comrades. In an instant an immense assembly was collected above our heads; it seemed as if a general attack was meditated, to drive us from our position. At a greater distance, various troops were heard, calling to, and answering one another. These hideous sounds, which at first made us laugh, soon became disagreeable in the extreme, and lasted, as near as I could guess, full two hours, till it decreased by degrees, and became more distant, and at last a dead stillness succeeded, such as commonly prevails in those woods.

Our simple evening meal was soon ready, and we sat down to our venison, of which the cook had made part into a curry, and roasted the rest. We did not want for seasoning, as the wild lemon and orange-trees grow in great plenty in the woods; and there was even one a few paces from our resting-place, on which we could see, by the light of our fire, the golden yellow fruit, glittering among the branches. While we were quietly occupied with our supper, we saw at a distance, through the trees, great troops of elephants approaching the brook. They kept a considerable distance from our fires, and passed on, contrary to their custom, in the quietest manner, like a herd of oxen. We heard them, at the same time, on the opposite side of the brook, and their tremendous roar re-echoed along the dark vault of the woods.

We judged it necessary to be upon our guard, as the elephants might be followed by much fiercer and more savage beasts. Our inclination to sleep left us, though we were extremely fatigued. We could not place much confidence in our koolies when on the watch; nor could we be greatly displeased with these good people, when we considered the heavy load all of them were obliged to carry upon their shoulders, and for the most part over a rough and unbeaten path. It was with difficulty that we could keep two of them awake sufficiently to attend the fires which burned around us.

Towards midnight we heard a great noise, and a shaking of the earth, as if a troop of wild animals were pursuing us at full speed. M. *D'Allemand* and I had the watch; we awoke the cooper and our people in haste; the baker we did not disturb, being afraid that, as he had drank more than did him good, he should be brought into danger by his foolish drunken tricks. Indeed, we now heartily repented our having any connexion with this man, who began to be uncommonly troublesome to us all, not only on account of his endless loquacity, with which he was continually interrupting our conversation, but still more from his constantly plaguing us for liquor, which we found extremely disagreeable. Besides, we found it very unpleasant to shout into his ears when we had any thing to say to him. We therefore let him lie; and scarcely had the cooper been awaked, when we heard, close behind us, a terrific, heart-piercing, and hideous roar, that issued from the mouth of an immense elephant, which we immediately discovered by the light of our fires, behind some trees; he stared at us without moving, turning his trunk so quickly round, and with so much force, that it occasioned a noise resembling that of the buzz of a spinning-wheel.

We made ready to welcome him with a discharge of our muskets; our guide, however, from a thick tree that he and the other koolies had ascended, conjured us not to fire, assuring us that it was a *Ronkedou*, which are extremely dangerous, and infinitely more to be dreaded than any other kind of elephants. It was, he continued, not probable that in the dark we could strike close behind the ear, the only place where he could be killed by a ball, as a wound in any other part of his body would only put him into a frightful rage, and cause him instantly to break in upon us. We knew not, however, how to rid ourselves of this troublesome guest. The package in which our rockets and flambeaus were, lay, unfortunately, not far from the dreadful animal, and any one that durst have ventured to bring it, would, without doubt, have exposed himself to certain death.

In this doubtful situation we thought of our cymbals, thinking they would undoubtedly drive him away; but scarcely had the sound of them reached his ears, when, uttering a dreadful roar, capable of filling the most courageous heart with terror, and at the same time, with inconceivable fury, twisting his trunk round a slender tree that stood near him, he tore it out of the earth, bent it several times together, and crushed it like a small plant under his feet. He then advanced slowly towards our post, doubtless with the intention of destroying every thing that came in his way. An irresistible movement made us hasten to save our baggage, and at the same time uttering a piercing shout, which was answered by our people from the tree, in a manner no less terrifying, as they thought us already devoted to destruction. This, accompanied with a sudden and tremendous clash of our cymbals, frightened the elephant so much that he at once turned round, and flapping his ears in a ludicrous manner, as a token that this concert was by no means agreeable to him, he fled so fast that he was instantly beyond the reach of the balls that we sent after him.

We were overjoyed to have got rid of this troublesome guest so happily, but at the same time we learned how little reliance could be placed upon our koolies in the time of need. We now divided the rockets and flambeaus among the men, that we might not in future be exposed to such dangers; as the wild beasts &c. especially the elephants, have an unconquerable dread of fire.

CHAPTER. V.

Arrival at Palliar—Pillie, aya!—Unfortunate Accident; our plan almost defeated—The decayed tree—Vedativé—Jovial company there—Manner of hunting of the Vedahs—Combat with a tiger—Arrival at Mantotte.

The next day we continued our journey without any accident. Towards evening we lighted our torches, and soon after came to a small plain or opening in the wood, in the middle of which we saw four elephants; on the appearance of our torches, our cimbals being sounded at the same time, they took to flight across the marshes. The road now became amazingly stony, and full of ruts and holes. Our guide then informed us that the mountains of *Caaragaking* were situated only a few miles to the left, and this was the occasion of the way being so rough and stony. At last we arrived, about nine o'clock, at a third lonely hut or ambalam, called *Palliar*, surrounded with trees of uncommon height and thickness.

I was so fatigued as to be scarcely able to stand. Being unaccustomed to such long journeys on foot, I felt in the morning the fatigues of the preceding day; my legs were stiff and swollen, and in a kind of benumbed state, which did not leave them till I had walked for some time, and the blood was brought into circulation. It was only, however, in the commencement that I suffered inconvenience from this; as we proceeded I became more inured to fatigue.

After our supper was finished, M. D'Allemand, who performed tolerably well upon the violin, began to play. The cooper and baker instantly began to dance. The baker, who had as usual drank rather too much, accompanied his dancing with such ludicrous skips and capers, that nobody could forbear laughing. The remark I made to my companions that he danced to the motion of the fiddle stick, and paid not the least attention to the music, furnished us with more food for merriment. At last they threw themselves upon their mats, overcome with fatigue, and soon fell sound asleep.

In the middle of the night the two koolies, with whom I had the watch, awoke me from a sort of reverie into which I had unconsciously fallen. The exclamation "Pillie, ayá" "a tiger, sir," from one of them, was, however, sufficient to rouse me in an instant. They pointed out to me at the same time two small glittering balls not far from one of the outer fires. I had no doubt they were the eyes of a tiger, at that moment on the watch to seize in the dark any of us who should remove from the fires. I awoke the cooper, as he was the best marksman, and we agreed to take aim exactly in the middle between the two flaming balls, and to fire at the same time. We fired, and for a few moments after a short quick movement was heard, like something struggling with death; it diminished by degrees, and at last entirely ceased.

It was laughable to see the fright in which our people, and particularly the baker, awoke out of their sleep. After having explained to them the cause of their surprise, we went to lie down a little longer; except the baker, who relieved me of the watch for the rest of the night.

The day had scarcely begun to dawn, when he awoke us with a joyful shout and the news that we had shot an uncommonly large tiger. He leaped and danced like a madman, and had already, with the assistance of the koolies, dragged the animal into the middle resting place. Both shots had taken place; one of them had shattered his head, and the other had entered his side. The cooper having an equal claim with me to the skin, which was beautifully striped, we agreed to cast lots for it: fortune favoured me, and after it was stripped from the carcase we pursued our journey.

From the near neighbourhood of the *Couragahing* mountains, our way was now scantily provided with trees, but at the same time extremely uneven, full of deep holes and clefts, and very rocky. The great multitude of ants' nests retarded our progress, as we were every moment obliged to avoid them, which rendered our journey still more difficult.

These ants are called *vay* by the inhabitants; they differ but little from the carias or white ants, which are found every where in India, except that they are larger. They make heaps or hillocks, some of which are from five to six feet high, and full ten paces in circumference; the top being of a conical shape. The earth or clay of which they are made is so hard, that it can scarcely be cut with a hatchet. This hardness is chiefly produced by a particular kind of moisture with which they mix and prepare the clay.

These obstacles rendered our progress so fatiguing that we resolved to direct our course to the *Couragahing* mountains, which lay not far to the eastward of us, as well with the hope of finding a better road, as with a view to gratify our curiosity. M. *D'Allemand* was in despair when he heard this decision, and endeavoured, but in vain, to make us change our resolution. An unfortunate and unexpected accident, however, to his great joy, accomplished that for which his eloquence had been exerted to no purpose.

After we had continued our course for some time towards the east, in order to reach the mountains of *Couragahing*, we observed by chance a nest of bees, of uncommonly large size, in a tree not very thickly covered with leaves. We would gladly have made ourselves masters of it, but the height of the branch from which it hung prevented us from expelling the bees by smoke, which is the usual method. We were therefore going to proceed on our way, when one of the koolies offered to climb up into the tree, and with a stroke or two of a hatchet, cut off the branch to which the said bees nest was attached, and had it fallen we could have easily expelled our little enemies with smoke. We accepted his offer and promised him a double share of the honey when we should become possessed of it.

He immediately sprung joyfully up the tree and soon reached the desired branch, but scarcely had he given a stroke with the hatchet, when the bees, before he had time for a second blow, attacked his naked body in such multitudes, and with such fury, that he began to howl in a strange manner, and with his eyes shut, endeavouring to descend the tree in haste, he made a false step, fell from a considerable height, with a most hideous yell, and broke his leg in a shocking manner. This accident deranged our whole plan; we could not leave this unfortunate man in the midst of the wilderness at the mercy of savage beasts, exposed to the horrors of dying of hunger and thirst. And even if we could have been so inhumanly cruel, his companions would have opposed our purpose and left us. We therefore, to the great joy of M. D'Allemand, came to the resolution to turn again to the west in search of inhabited places.

We placed the wounded man upon a sort of litter, hastily constructed of the branches of trees, on which he could be carried without too much motion. We then divided his share of the baggage, and that of the two koolies who were to carry him, among the rest, and bent the course of our journey with all the speed possible towards the west. It was then ten o'clock in the morning, and we hoped before the close of the day to fall in with a Dutch post or settlement.

With this view we took in great haste, but with much difficulty, the direction of the shore; we were constantly obliged to cut our way through the bushes. The more we advanced towards the west, the woods became the thicker and more impassable. M. D'Allemand seemed to feel a savage joy at the accident which had befallen the poor kooly, as we were obliged by it to return to inhabited places. He blessed the bees, and proposed to write a poem in praise of their courage; but he was, not long after, punished for his want of feeling and ill-timed mirth.

Having for some time annoyed us with expressing the happiness he felt, he attempted, in the fulness of his joy, to leap upon the trunk of a decayed tree which lay across the path; but no sooner had his feet touched the bark than he sank in it almost up to the middle. His sudden immersion made us all burst out into a loud laugh. With difficulty we delivered him from his captivity, and after he was cleansed from the dust and rubbish, we requested him to compose a poetical eulogium upon old decayed trees; from which, however, with much politeness, he begged to be excused. He escaped for this time with a fright, but it might have ended fatally for him, as a particular kind of serpents, and venomous spiders of a prodigious size, frequently take up their abode in the trunks of such decayed and rotten trees.

About one o'clock in the afternoon, we came to a small open space or plain, the surface of which was soft and muddy. We found here many skeletons of elephants. After passing along one side of this morass, we took a hearty refreshment under a large talpat-tree, having no time for a regular meal.

We again resumed our journey, and some time after, not far from us, we saw a bear preparing to ascend a tree, but upon our approach, he disappeared among the bushes. We observed that he had intended to regale himself with the *palpalum*, or milk-fruit, which sort of trees abounded in this wood. The fruit in shape and size greatly resembles the olive, and conceals under a thin yellow rind, a white gluey moisture, very sweet, with the taste of cream: The bears and wild boars are extremely fond of this fruit; the natives dry it in the sun, when it has nearly the taste of raisins.

We saw here great numbers of wild swine, but they were uncommonly shy and cautious. I had never seen them before but in troops, running always at full gallop, and continually grunting, with their young ones in the middle of the troop. They are not so large as those of the northern part of the island, and I question much if they are so fierce.

The complaints and lamentations of our poor kooly, the detestable road, and particularly the want of water, having met with nothing but stagnant and muddy pools, made us wish heartily to fall in with an inhabited place.

At eight o'clock in the evening, to our great joy, we emerged f om those immense woods and entered upon a large plain, covered with elephants' dung, though we saw none of those animals. About ten o'clock we came to *Vedativé*, a large village, being the first place since our departure from *Panorin*, where we had seen human beings. As soon as we arrived we sent for the commanding serjeant, who placed our kooly in the hands of a potter.

The Indian potters, besides their usual occupation, practise as surgeons in curing sprains, reducing dislocations, and setting broken bones, at which they are very expert and skilful. Besides the usual previous prayers and conjurations, they make use of certain plants, that they find in the woods, the knowledge of which remains a secret, except to their own cast. As soon as the herbs are applied to the wound, the prayers and incantations are repeated, no doubt to inspire the patient with greater confidence in their remedy, and to give a high idea of their abilities. An Indian is every where superstitious; he is firmly persuaded that a pandian or physician, who accompanies his medicine with prayers and conjurations, is infinitely more learned than the waitam, who cures with herbs only.

After having supplied our poor kooly with some money, we followed the serjeant to his hut. We found there a great company; four young girls, and three Mestese women with their husbands, were sitting before the door under a large tamarind-tree, enjoying themselves by accompanying the sound of a Rabanna or Indian lute with their voices. The serjeant informed us that he was giving a little family feast; his daughter, having the week before been married to a young man at *Manar*, had, with her husband, come to pay him a visit. He introduced us to them as well as to his wife, his sister, and her husband; two of the young girls were his own daughters, and the other two his brother's.

They immediately presented us with vellapatty, a sort of very strong arrack, distilled from palm-wine and the bark of a certain tree, which gives it a very unpleasant smell, much like that of bugs. We durst not refuse this detestable liquor, and still less make use of our own; as, if they had had the least suspicion that we were provided with wine and other good liquors, we should certainly very soon not have had a drop remaining. After this a supper was served up, which in some measure restored our stomachs from the bad effects of the abominable liquor we had been obliged to swallow. It consisted of rice and most excellent venison; every one had his dish placed upon his knee, and we supped with the greatest satisfaction. During the repast our kind host informed us that he was only a corporal with a serjeant's pay, and had six tapaz soldiers under his command; that his duty consisted in nothing more than to let out some salt-pans a little distance from the village, and to receive the company's dues and tolls from the inhabitants; that *Vedativé* was in the government of *Jaffnapatnam*; that his name was *Jan Voet*, and his grandfather had passed the whole of his life at this post, as well as his father, since whose death he had spent twenty years here; that he was a cartier, and a great lover of hunting. All this was related with so much ingenuousness and good humour, that I could not forbear from secretly envying this man, to whom it never seemed to have occurred, that he was no better than an exile here, in a place where his forefathers had before ended their days, and who was not, like me, driven about the world by a restless disposition. Among other things he gave me a description of his manner of hunting, which is the same that the Vaddahs use. It occasions no fatigue whatever, and is attended with very little danger.

Near the side of any large pond, a hole is dug four feet deep, and wide enough for two or three persons to sit in; this hole, particularly on the side next the water, is covered with leaves, branches, and earth, leaving only a small opening to shoot through, and to see what takes place. Towards night the hunters hide themselves in these holes and watch the wild beasts that come out of the woods to quench their thirst.

I have been informed by many persons that animals of every species come to drink in different herds or droves. The elephants always come first, and stay longest, as they usually bathe themselves before drinking, and when the water is not deep enough, they draw it up into their trunks and refresh themselves by spouting it over their bodies. The buffaloes arrive next; after having quenched their thirst, they amuse themselves by lying down in the water, and playing and tumbling about in it. The tigers also and the bears have their turns, and at last towards morning, the wild swine, deer, and other sorts. It is then that the hunters take their aim, and firing among the crowd bring down great numbers of every kind.

This manner of hunting is not, however, altogether free from danger. It sometimes happens that the wild beasts, and particularly the tigers and wild buffaloes, discover the hunters, either by the scent, or by happening to come out of the water on the same side where they are concealed. There are even instances of elephants having fallen into the pits, and crushed the people within them. To avoid such misfortunes as much as possible, the hunters always go in parties of three or four together, one of whom has his attention fixed on the opposite side of the water, to warn the others, and to drive away the beasts that approach too near, by firing upon them or throwing their rockets. But sometimes the greatest vigilance is unavailing, especially if the water is in the middle of a thick wood, because an elephant, when he walks slowly, has so soft a step that he is not heard till very near.

But to return to the singular order that seems to prevail among the inhabitants of the woods: though I do not believe it is so regular as it is sometimes represented to be, yet it is certain that the instinct or natural powers of the weaker animals teaches them not to approach the water before the break of day, when their enemies, satiated with prey, return to their dens.

When supper was over, one of the company again took up the *rabanna*, but M. *D'Allemand*, who was little entertained with its music, had privately ordered his slave to surprise them with his violin. The sound of the instrument no sooner reached their ears, than they all seemed as if struck by an electrical shock. They all stood up, and the young girls, encouraged by the example of their parents, eagerly called for a country dance, and taking us by the hand, notwithstanding our objections and protestations of being fatigued, they drew us into the circle. All, even to the old corporal and his wife, joined in the dance. The baker, who was quite beside himself with joy, kept the company in a continual roar of laughter, with his capers and grimaces. Without having seen his ludicrous features it is impossible to form an idea of the extravagant and ridiculous forms into which he distorted his countenance, and for which, indeed, his face and his whole person were singularly adapted—he was truly an original.

After dancing some time, we found ourselves incapable, from fatigue, to hold out any longer; and we sat down before the hut. The rest of the company having also finished, came and placed themselves by us, and began to sing a sort of Malabar love songs, called *chicotics* and *chacras*. As I excelled in that kind of singing, I received the applause of the whole company. My companions, who did not understand a word of the songs, and still less could sing them, stared at me with admiration, and the respect of my Koolies, who had listened at some distance, rose from that moment in a remarkable degree.

Towards morning we spread our mats in a remote corner of the hut and enjoyed a short repose. Our Koolies awoke us at day-break, and we soon after departed, without awaking our host, whom we had taken leave of the night before.

It was about half an hour before sun-rise when we set out. We passed in the beginning over a large plain, interspersed here and there with Cocoa and wild Palm-trees, the ground was intersected by small rivulets, the water of which we found brackish.

About nine o'clock we came to a great standing pool, surrounded with high and thick bushes. From a small sand hill on which we stood, we could see that the water was covered with such innumerable multitudes of birds, as ducks, geese, snipes, &c. that the surface could scarcely be seen. We were very desirous to provide ourselves with a good dinner among them, as we had begun to get tired of the venison. M. *D'Allemand* offered to scramble through the bushes, and when he had got to the edge of the pool, to fire at the birds, and as they flew up we should also take aim at them. No sooner said than done.—M. D'Allemand crept into the bushes and soon disappeared among them. In the mean time we stood impatiently waiting for the shot; but in vain. We heard nothing, though he might have been long at the appointed place. We now became anxious, and prepared to penetrate in a body through the bushes he had entered, when, to our great surprize, we saw him rushing with the utmost speed out of the brambles, and making haste towards us, without his hat and gun. Terror and dismay were painted upon his countenance, and he was almost out of breath. He told us that having with much difficulty got through the thorns and bushes, and come to the place, where he intended to surprise the birds ; just when about to fire, he heard the snorting of an animal, and turning round saw a tiger of immense size asleep, surrounded with bloody and half-gnawed bones. Seized with terror and alarm, he endeavoured to return as softly as possible ; but scarcely had he taken a few steps when he heard the tiger move. Almost giving himself up for lost, he had thrown away his gun that he might the more easily escape. Such was the account he gave of his adventure. We might now have continued our journey, but the gun was much too necessary an article to be lost in such a manner, which, with his hat, remained hanging among the bushes. We therefore resolved to expel the tiger, and for this purpose made a tremendous noise with our cymbals, and threw a rocket at the spot pointed out by M. *D'Allemand.* The animal instantly rushed furiously out, but apparently not having expected to find so many people, he stood suddenly still, and seemed undecided what to do; when, thinking to frighten him, we advanced upon him armed with our pistols and pikes. But instead of taking to flight at our approach as we expected, he went very slowly to a small eminence on which he placed himself, without showing the smallest appearance of fear ; then turning towards us, he showed his large snow-white teeth, and glaring frightfully at us, he bent up his body in an extraordinary manner, while his long hair stood erect like bristles, giving the whole animal a most terrific appearance.

This attitude damped our courage extremely, and we all deemed it more prudent to attack him from a distance, except the baker, whom we could with difficulty prevent from charging him with his long sword. We then sent him two rockets, the last of which whizzed past so close to his nose, that he sprang on one side with his tail drawn in, and fled howling with all his might.

After having dislodged our unwelcome guest, we went to explore the bushes, where we found the hat, hanging upon a branch, and a little farther the gun. Coming to the place where M. D'Allemand first saw the tiger, we found it strewed with the bones of various animals. The still bloody head of a large ape, which we observed among the rest, made us suppose that he had made his last meal of the body. Our guide assured us, however, that the tiger has an aversion to the flesh of apes, and never eats it ; except when compelled by necessity, or as a medicine when sick ; but he could not inform me what species of ape is selected for this purpose.

This occurrence, while it convinced us of the utility of our rockets, taught us at the same time, never to lay aside our hunting knives, or cutlasses, which M. D'Allemand had done in order to penetrate the more easily through the thickets. The tiger had probably been in a kind of lethargy or inactivity, either from being surfeited with prey or from indisposition; but how easily might he have attacked M. D'Allemand, with what could he have defended himself? His gun loaded with swan-shot, would have had little effect upon so fierce an animal; his escape was therefore extremely fortunate.

Having taken our road through sand, we came at two o'clock to *Mantotte*, a large and beautiful village not far from the island of *Manar*. The company here maintains a Malabar *Adigaar*,* who has some Peons under him. We lodged in a large church, built by the Portuguese; it now serves as a resting place for travellers. The body of this building appeared to be in good repair, though consisting only of bricks; the doors and windows had been taken away.

As provisions had begun to fail us, and we could find none in this village, I sent a Kooly with a letter to Mr. *Nagel*, engineer at *Manar*, with whom I was intimately acquainted, requesting him to send us some provisions and bottles of wine, for which we would pay him. In the interval we made ready our kitchen in the church, as many had apparently done before us, one side of the wall being quite black with smoke. Our dinner consisted of some partridges and wild-fowl, which we had shot by the way.

Our Kooly returned at seven o'clock in the evening; he brought us six bottles of arrack, and two of a sort of brandy, besides some provisions. Mr. Nagel answered me that he was very sorry he could not provide us better, necessaries being exceedingly scarce even on the island, as a company of Malays that had been sent to reinforce the garrison of *Jaffnapatnam* had consumed the grerate part, and taken the remainder with them, and a sloop which was expected every day from Colombo was not yet arrived; he had sent me as much liquor and provisions from his own store as he could spare, which he hoped I would accept of.

As we had slept but little the night before at *Vedativé*, we resolved to remain all night here, to sleep off the fatigues of our journey, in order that we might be able to renew it with fresh vigour.

---

* Inspector or overseer; he is at the same time chief magistrate of the village.

CHAPTER VI.

Bangala — Unpleasant adventure there—The Brahmin of Calaar —Furious engagement between two wild buffaloes — Dangerous occurrence — Departure— Morgam —The tiger scent—Disagreeable halting place.

The next morning at five o'clock we again set forward, taking our course over a great sandy plain. The jackals, though found in every part of the forest, seemed to have established their head-quarters here; we saw great numbers running about, which concealed themselves in the woods on our approach. We here killed a serpent, which our people called *Gorunda;* it was quite green, about four feet long, and from three to four inches thick. The deep and hot sand on the beach made our progress very difficult, and we hastened to reach a clump of wild palm-trees, which we saw at a distance, that we might rest a little and take our breakfast. We found there two Malabar travellers, who told us, they had left *Chilaw* two days before, and were going to *Manaar*. We learned from them, among other things, that a *French Caré*, or Frenchman, who had come in a palanquin from Colombo by Poetlan, had been killed by an elephant, and that higher up the roads were entirely overrun by those animals.

The great forest still continued on our left, and stretching along the whole extent of the horizon. The plain was now better provided with trees, but the ground still consisted of rough sand. Clumps of palm or cocoa-trees were spread here and there, under which we sought protection from the burning rays of the sun. At last, about five o'clock, we reached *Bangala*, a large village, situated on the river of the same name, and for the most part inhabited by black christians of the Roman Catholic persuasion. We found here an ambelam it is true, but so small, so dirty, and at the same time so full of travellers, that, by virtue of our *oppa* or order we demanded of the Majoral to provide us with better lodgings.

He replied that this could not be accomplished without great difficulty; it might be done readily enough for one person, but for four of us and a Kooly to prepare our victuals, a whole hut was not sufficient; and besides, there were none empty; but to satisfy us he would make further enquiry.

He then left us, but soon returning, said, it was just as he expected with regard to the habitations, but that he had obtained the consent of the beadle that we might pass the night in the church, if we would promise not to damage it, and to light our fire under a sort of shed at a little distance. He then conducted us to our sacred quarters, which might be about a thousand yards from the village, where we found a dumb Indian, who appeared to be the beadle of whom the Majoral had spoken. He offered us his services by signs, and set before us excellent fish, milk, fruit, and all that the place could afford. The church was a small building; at one end was an altar with a wretched wooden image of the Virgin and Child over it. It was, besides, so black from the multitude of flies in it, that the real colour could not be distinguished. The pastor of this black congregation was absent at *Manaar*, from whence he was expected to return in a few days.

Every thing was ready next day for our departure, when we found that M. D'Allemand was absent. We all supposed he had taken a walk in to the village, or along the side of the river, and therefore dispatched one of our people to inform him that we were ready. Our messenger, however, did not return either, and it was not till I was going towards the village in search of them, that our messenger came running, out of breath, and told us that the French *Parengui*, or gentleman, was detained by the inhabitants of the village, who had tied his hands behind his back, and were going to conduct him to *Manaar*.

I stood for some time speechless with astonishment, and could by no means comprehend what could be the meaning of this strange occurrence. I called the cooper in haste, and having, in a few words, told him what had happened, we hastened towards the village, to learn the cause of this singular proceeding. We there found our fellow traveller in the midst of a great number of the natives, his hands bound behind his back, his face covered with blood, and with his clothes torn and hanging in rags from his body.

The crowd immediately made way for us, when, having called the Majoral, I demanded by what authority he detained travellers, and allowed them to be abused in such a manner, or if he called this obedience to the orders of the oppa, by affording travellers assistance and support?

He replied, that this *vallecaren*, or white man, had entered a hut by force, and not only abused a poor dumb man, but had besides set fire to the roof of his hut, which, from the wind blowing very high, might have laid the whole village in ashes, had not some people, whom the uproar had collected, extinguished the fire, and prevented him from further violence. As for what concerned himself, (the Majoral,) he had obeyed the oppa, even more than he was obliged to do, and had supplied us with the best the place could afford, at a very moderate price; but the oppa gave us no right to abuse people, and set fire to their houses, and he would send the prisoner to *Manaar*, that he might be punished according to law.

I was greatly disturbed at these words, which the Majoral delivered with a very decided tone and manner; and, with an angry look, turning to my captive fellow traveller, I asked what infernal spirit had tempted him to inveigle us into so disagreeable a situation, and to delay our journey with his mad freaks, because, as he was found in our company, we should be obliged to follow him to *Manaar*, and wait there till he should be tried. He answered that the dumb beadle was the sole cause of all that had happened, having promised, by signs, to bring him a mistress the night before, for which he had given him two pagodas beforehand; but the rascal had not kept his word, and had kept out of the way. He had, therefore, gone to his hut in search of him, to punish him for his deceit, and get back his money; but growing furious from not being able to satisfy his revenge, he had, in his rage, set fire to the roof of the rascal's hut, without reflecting at the moment of the fatal consequences that might have followed so inconsiderate an action; upon this he was laid hold of and abused by the people.

I took the Majoral aside, and warned him to consider well what he was going to do; that this vallecaren, or *white man*, was a friend of Mr. Noy, the commandant of Manaar, and was, besides, charged with dispatches of the utmost importance, which he was obliged to deliver personally into the hands of the Governor of Colombo; and that he, (the majoral) would have to answer for all the unnecessary delay he might occasion in our journey. I shewed him besides, that the offence was not so great, and that the dumb man had been the principal cause of it himself, whom it by no means became, as a person belonging to the church, to rob travellers of their money, under pretence of bringing women to them in the night; of which scandalous conduct I should inform the priest without delay, who would no doubt punish him according to his deserts. "I therefore advise you as a friend," continued I, "to let the prisoner go, and be content with a suitable compensation, sufficient to repair the dumb man's hut, and in some degree remunerate him for the blows he has received."

At first he would by no means agree to this proposal, but after long persuasion, and much talking on both sides, I at last obtained the release of my companion, whom this adventure cost eight pagodas, besides having his clothes torn to rags, and a prodigious number of blows.

We now made haste to quit this fatal spot, lest they should change their mind, and leaving the path, we entered a thick wood, where we made our way with great difficulty. When we supposed ourselves out of the reach of danger, M. D'Allemand gave us a detail of the circumstances which had given rise to the whole affair.

He had the preceding night, by signs, asked the dumb man if he could procure a female companion for him, to which, after making some difficulty, he consented, making our fellow traveller understand, that as soon as we were asleep he was to get up and go to an old uninhabited hut, which he shewed him; (this might easily be done, as the church remained open all night,) and he would there bring him a very pretty girl, whom he even pointed out to him, as she happened to pass by at the time. For this he was to receive three pagodas, two of which were to be paid in advance.

Our credulous companion relying upon the promise of this cheat, had waited the whole night in the above-mentioned hut, till at last, at break of day, finding he had been deceived by this rascal, and furious at having lost his money and night's rest, he, accompanied by his slave, repaired to the village with the intention of punishing the dumb beadle for his treachery, and recover the money he had given him. After having with much difficulty found out the hut, he went in, and found the dumb man in company with two other persons. As soon as the former saw him he endeavoured to make his escape, but our enraged fellow-traveller, cutting off his retreat, seized him by the breast, threw him on the ground, and began to belabour him so effectually, with a stick he had brought with him on purpose, that he uttered the most hideous and ridiculous yells that can possibly be imagined.

The two other men had allowed all this to pass in silence, and were apparently filled with astonishment, but seeing their companion treated in such a manner, they now flew to his assistance. One of them attacked the enemy behind, throwing his blows most powerfully upon his back with an iron rod, in order to force him to let go his prey; while the other struggled with the slave, who endeavoured to assist his master.

Our comrade then got up to return his adversary's blows with interest, but finding him prepared, upon the least motion, to split his head with the iron rod, he, without knowing at the moment what he did, took a burning faggot from the fire, and thrust it into the roof of the hut, which being of palm-leaves, instantly began to burn. Some people collected by the disturbance were, however, fortunate enough to extinguish the flames; but at the same time making themselves masters of him and his slave, they were brought, after being terribly abused, before the Majoral, who would have sent them to *Manaar* as rioters and incendiaries, if we had not come in time to prevent him.

Notwithstanding that we considered him as already sufficiently punished for his imprudence, we could not avoid expressing our dissatisfaction at his conduct, which might have led to fatal consequences, and had occasioned considerable delay in our journey.

We again got quickly out of the wood, and proceeded over a sandy plain, covered with bushes and brambles, without a single tree capable of defending us from the burning rays of the sun. At last, to our no small joy, we came to *Aripo*, a small fort with two bulwarks, built by the Portuguese. The Company maintains here a small garrison, consisting of a corporal and some invalids, who all lodge in the village, probably being afraid of being buried under the ruins of the old walls. No other provisions could be procured here but fish, which, however, was excellent, and very cheap. The fish are caught in a river that runs close to the village, and is called *Coumda*. It rises among the mountains of *Cauragahing*, and flows past the port of Aripo into the sea. In other respects, however cheerful it might formerly have been, in the time of the pearl fishery, it was then a desert, barren, and melancholy place.

About three o'clock in the afternoon, we again commenced our journey. Our way now ran along the sea-coast, upon a dyke formed by nature. We came to the place upon the plain, where, during the pearl-fishing season, the oysters are brought, and shut up in inclosures, and where they are also opened. We found here several women and children busy in fanning and sifting the sand, for the purpose of finding any pearls that might have been left at the last fishing. I was told that these people are sometimes fortunate enough to find pearls of considerable value.

We still pursued our journey along the sea-shore, which was strewed with a multitude of beautiful shells, sponges, &c. On the left we had a great and extensive forest, full of high and thick trees, and stretching down to the shore, and sometimes to within a few yards of the sea. In the mean while our way became more and more difficult as we proceeded. We were every now and then obliged to make a circuit, sometimes into the country to avoid a reef of rocks, the sharp points of which rose from two to three feet above the sand; then again we were under the necessity of wading breast-high in the sea, to get round the completely impenetrable tall thorns and bushes, which sometimes extended from the wood ten or twelve yards into the sea.

These difficulties soon made us repent of having left the inland road, and we resolved to leave the shore and strike again into the woods. But here also we travelled with great difficulty: we had to struggle with a deep rough sand, full of thorns and brambles, which continually obstructed our passage, without taking into account a number of other obstacles, which are commonly met with in untrodden or unfrequented paths. This part of the wood swarmed with elks and other animals of that species. We also saw the traces of wild buffaloes, and even the marks of a tiger, leopard, or other wild beast of that kind. We were every moment startled by deer, which at our approach sprung out of the bushes, and fled with astonishing swiftness.

It was about seven o'clock when we reached *Calaar*, which was almost dried up, and over whose naked and rocky bed we approached an Indian pagoda, situated on the opposite side, and also bearing the name of Calaar.

This river, which was then so much diminished, is in the rainy season filled to the brim in the course of a few hours, by the streams from the mountains; it was more than a thousand paces broad where we passed. It takes its rise in the mountains of *Cauragahing*, and after a long and very circuitous course, it loses itself among the mountains of *Grudumale*.

The brahmin of Calaar received us with great cordiality and affection, and placed before us milk tayer, dried palpalam, and another wild fruit, which he called *pergodhé*, and which has a great semblance to the *Atta*.*

We took up our quarters under two large trees that stood before the pagoda, though to the visible dissatisfaction of the Brahmin, who told us the trees were holy and consecrated to the divinity; but seeing that we preferred this spot to an old dirty hut, which he had repeatedly offered us, he remained silent, only begging us to kindle our fire at some distance, that we might not damage them. He called these trees *Bogaya*.†

This man having remarked that we were obliged to shout with all our might into the baker's ears to make ourselves understood, offered to cure him of his deafness, providing he would offer a black fowl to the Divinity of the pagoda, and allow a few drops of oil from a lamp that burned before his image to be poured into his ears.

I imparted this proposal to our deaf baker, and if we had not prevented him, he would have submitted to the experiment; but I looked upon it as a kind of humiliation and insult to the hhristian religion, and was besides firmly persu ided that it would ave no effect whatever.

The Brahmin, whom we found to be a friendly and communicative man, was by no means offended at the refusal of our fellow traveller to put confidence in his remedy. He seemed quite overjoyed to have found in me a person that could converse

* The *Atta* is a sort of apple, the rind of which is hard and of a greyish green colour; it is white and soft within like marmalade, is eaten with a spoon, and has a sweet and agreeable taste when fully ripe. It has a great resemblance to a medlar, but is whiter and of a more beautiful appearance.

* A tree the branch of which tumbles incessantly; it is highly venerated by the Indians on a religious account.

with him in his own language. Among other things I inquired to what cause it was owing that this temple had been erected in a place so solitary and remote, and so distant from all habitations. He then related the following story or fable.

A *Modeliaar** was attacked on this spot by a *Pambourajah*, or royal serpent, of a dreadful size ; in danger of being instantly devoured, he ejaculated a prayer to the goddess *Rhadakistna* for her assistance. Upon this a woman of a most beautiful form appeared, with loose flowing hair, one of which she plucked out, which was instantly changed into a sword, with which she instantly cut off the serpent's head and then vanished into the air. From gratitude for this timely assistance, he had caused to be erected on the same spot this temple, which is still annually visited by pilgrims from all parts.

Though the bed of the river was quite bare, there were here and there several deep places in which the water remained. These ponds or pools, from the rich moisture of the earth, and the amazing quickness with which weeds as well as fruits shoot up in those countries, were almost all surrounded with high and thick bushes or underwood. This was remarked by the cooper when we arrived, and at the same time recollecting what the commander of the fort of *Vedativé* had told us of his manner of hunting, he proposed that we should conceal ourselves in the thickets and bushes that encircled the pools, and watch the animals that should come to quench their thirst. This proposal was made with no other view than to satisfy his unbounded passion for sport, as we were abundantly provided with all sorts of game. He had in fact supplied us with much more than we wanted, as he did nothing on the way but shoot at every animal and bird that made its appearance, indifferent whether it could be made use of or was at all eatable. This practice gave rise to a great many disputes between him and me, as I hold nothing to be more cruel, contemptible, or unworthy, than to kill a harmless unsuspecting animal merely for amusement, or for the empty praise of being what is calleda good shot.

I therefore decidedly refused to be of the party, and endeavoured to convince him, as well as M. D'Allemand, of the danger to which they would expose themselves ; even the brahmin persuaded them against it, but all in vain. At last, finding that I remained stedfast in my resolution, they begged I would at least accompany them, to assist and support them if it should be necessary.

To this I in the end consented, after having made another fruitless attempt to persuade them from this foolish undertaking.

---

*A person of high consideration; a general or commander of the troops.

All that I could obtain from them was, that they would not set out till towards day break, as the largest and fiercest animals would then have retired and given place to the smaller sorts which came only in the morning, if our host at *Vedativé* had told us the truth. By following this plan the danger of engaging with elephants, tigers, buffaloes, and other savage beasts might be avoided. To this they consented, and we all lay down to take some rest, except the cooper's slave-boy and a kooly, who were to keep the watch and awake us at four o'clock.

In the midst of a sound sleep I was awoke by a voice calling out,—"Up ! up !—it is time, get up—the day will soon break." It was just two o'clock, and the cooper could wait no longer, so that in spite of all I could say we were obliged to set out. The baker would not go with us, and we were heartily glad of it.

Before our departure we loaded our pieces and filled our pouches with cartridges. We now wandered slowly along the bed of the river—At a distance on the other side, the noise of animals echoed deep and terrible through the forest; we heard in almost every watery place around us, rustling and motion. We agreed to watch at one of the largest, and crept as softly as possible, at a few paces distant from each other, into the bushes and thorns, with which it was surrounded. This pool seemed to be about four hundred paces in circumference. My companions had promised not to fire at an elephant or any other fierce beast, but to wait patiently the arrival of the smaller animals.

We had not been long concealed in our thorny hiding-place, when we observed two animals on the other side of the water, busy in quenching their thirst. The moon at that moment was covered by a thick cloud, so that I could not distinguish what they were. It is certain, however, they belonged to the tiger species, though somewhat smaller. As soon as they had drank, which they did the one after the other, and not at the same time, though there was sufficient space, they set off at full speed for the woods.

Another half hour nearly elapsed without any more animals making their appearance, but the noise resounding on all sides made me very uneasy. I kept looking anxiously round me, afraid every moment of being fallen upon by a tiger, a serpent, or some such creature. My companions became also uneasy, and heartily wished themselves safe at the Pagoda. At last we heard the deep low of some approaching animals, which we soon distinguished to be three buffaloes.

After having drank a long time, they waded into the water till it was above their belly, then lay down in it, so that nothing could be seen but their noses. They remained in this position close to one another, for nearly a quarter of an hour, and any one who had not seen them go into the water, would never have at all suspected that such heavy unwieldy animals were concealed below the surface.

A fourth buffalo now made his appearance, and after snuffing very strongly at every thing round him, he also began to drink. The others had thrust their heads out of the water, when he approached, but did not seem willing to hinder him from drinking. Having quenched his thirst, he appeared inclined to join the rest in the water, but no sooner had one of the three observed this, than he stood up, and instantly attacked him with a hideous roar. The sky was at this time free from clouds, and the moon shone in all her brightness, so that I had the satisfaction of beholding this terrible combat very plainly. I by no means regretted having joined this hunting party. To see two such furious animals fight at so short a distance, is certainly an interesting spectacle.

The rage and might with which they attacked each other is not to be described.---At every charge they retired some steps backwards, making the sand fly in clouds behind, and with dreadful snortings, they rushed at full speed, with the swiftness of an arrow, upon each other, so that they recoiled some paces back from the concussion. Sometimes, after having quickly approached each other, they suddenly stopped for an instant, till, bending their heads to the ground at the same time, the combat was again renewed. By degrees the open space between them became shorter; and blow followed blow in rapid succession, with a dreadful clatter, that was echoed and re-echoed along both sides of the woody banks.

During this furious strife, the two others, which no doubt were females, lay quietly in the water; they only now and then turned their heads towards the place where the fortune of war was to decide to which of the two combatants, that seemed to be bulls, they should belong.

At last, the one that arrived first was lucky enough to give the other such a tremendous blow in the side, that, without waiting for a second, he left the field of battle, and fled with the utmost speed into the forest.

The proud conqueror, without pursuing his enemy, having lowed twice with so clear and terrific a sound that the echo resounded on every side, again betook himself to the water with the two others.

Notwithstanding the terror occasioned by the combat between these furious and enraged animals, it was a gratification to me to be present at so grand a spectacle, and I awaited impatiently for the arrival of another buffalo, that I might have the pleasure of seeing it renewed.—But how great was my terror when, in place of this, I heard a gun go off.

The buffaloes stood altogether, snorting terribly; the bull and another instantly rushed through the water towards the side where they had seen the flash, while the third came out on the opposite side, to go round the bushes, and fall upon the enemy in the rear.

Full of terror and dismay, I endeavoured to get out of the bushes before the dreadful animal could come round to where I was, but, unfortunately, (I cannot think of it even now without horror,) my long hair got entangled among the thorns, for I had lost my hat, and it was impossible to extricate it in time. I already heard the furious enraged animal coming; by a tremendous effort I tore myself loose, with so much violence, that my head struck against the gravel, and a great part of my hair remained sticking in the brambles. I instantly began to run, in order, if possible, to reach the Pagoda, which stood at two hundred yards distance.—In vain;—terror had deprived me of my faculties;—It was with me like one who dreams that he is fleeing to avoid a pursuer; he imagines that his limbs are nailed to the ground, or that an invisible power detains him—terror-struck, and with a beating heart, in vain he puts forth all his strength, he is withheld by an irresistible hand.

The furious beast was now close upon me; already I was affected by his breath;—I looked round, he was not six paces distant; the thought struck me like a flash of lightning, that the buffaloes, when they have approached near enough to their enemy, run at him with their heads bent down to the ground, and he who has sufficient presence of mind to spring aside at the moment when the animal aims a blow at him, will save himself, as the beast cannot halt instantly; and besides, it is not the nature of the buffalo to turn back and attack his enemy anew.

But this method could be of no use to me; my pursuer was already too near me: instead of it, at the moment when ready to become his prey, I threw myself on the ground at full length, and the next moment the furious beast ran over me at full speed. What a narrow escape I had made! His hind feet were scarcely a span distant from my head, and I was entirely covered with the sand which he threw up behind him like a cloud.

As soon as he was past, I had the presence of mind to creep upon my hands and knees under a neighbouring thicket. I remained here, trembling, and in the greatest perplexity, till, to my unspeakable joy, I heard the voices of my companions, who were in search of me, armed with burning pieces of wood. Upon my calling they all came towards me. It was with a good deal of difficulty they extricated me from my hiding-place, and they were quite astonished how it had been possible for me to penetrate so far into the thicket. The shouts of the cooper and M. D'Allermand had awakened the Brahmin and all his family, as well as the koolies. I had been missed, and as they found I did not arrive, they were afraid that I had been destroyed by one of those animals, or at least in great danger of my life. It may easily be supposed that I was greatly incensed against them, as it was by their imprudence I had been exposed to an almost inevitable death. They were not to blame, however; a branch of thorn had, without their knowledge, struck the lock of the cooper's gun, which was full-cocked; at least he gave this as an excuse.

Next day I felt myself indisposed with a violent head-ache and slight fever. We remained till mid-day, and though I did not find myself much better, I thought it advisable to reach *Poetlan* by short stages, rather than to fall ill in such a solitary wilderness, where I might perish for want of remedies and assistance.

We therefore departed about three o'clock in the afternoon; our path lay through a thick wood of high trees, very full of leaves; it was uncommonly beautiful, free from underwood, weeds, and brambles, with which those forests are generally overgrown. We saw small herds of deer and elks grazing among the trees. I also remarked among the various kinds of apes that played among the branches, some which were perfectly black, with a white beard, which gave them a singularly solemn and venerable appearance. Our people called them *Wandroe.* We found here many traces of elephants and buffaloes, and here and there, among the other high trees, palms and cocoas, which induced me to believe that this place must have formerly been inhabited.

About seven in the evening we arrived at *Morgam*, a small place, where poverty and wretchedness seemed to prevail. We took up our quarters at the side of a well, where we found tolerably good water. The inhabitants had scarcely anything to eat, except a little *tinné*, a kind of yellow grain, having the shape and appearance of wheat. We passed a very disagreeable night, on account of the heavy rain, which did not cease till towards morning.

We re-commenced our journey as soon as the sun rose, being afraid of falling in with elephants, all the marks of which we had not only seen the day before, but had heard their roaring during the whole of the night. This also agreed with the information we received from the inhabitants, who advised us not to set out too early.

Near mid-day we reached a large open space of ground in the middle of the forest, where we proposed to halt for some time, as we found there a tolerably large well; but, to our great surprise, all our ropes joined together could not reach the water, though considerably upwards of thirty fathoms in length. At no great distance stood the ruins of a church, which had formerly belonged to the Portuguese, surrounded with brambles and underwood. One side had fallen in; and the fear of serpents and other reptiles, which are fond of making such ruinous places their abode, prevented us from examining the interior of it. Whilst we were at dinner, we saw two bears about a hundred paces from us: they passed by with a stately tread, and without showing the least signs of fear; they even stood still for some moments to look at us. Fortunately, they soon disappeared behind some bushes, as the cooper and M. D'Allegand had begun to load their guns, and we should probably have had new adventures, as these animals are by no means easily put to flight, and are any thing but accommodating.

At three o'clock we again set out. The wood was still full of large trees, but not so open and free; we were particularly troubled with multitudes of black ants, which were in most of the trees, and upon the least motion of the branches, fell upon us by hundreds. Their bite, which was very sharp, brought out a great many small pimples that occasioned an insufferable itching; the naked bodies of our poor Koolies were particularly exposed to it.

While we were thus making our way with great difficulty, our people, who formed a kind of advanced guard before us, turned back in great haste and warned us to be upon the look out, as they had smelled a tiger which could not be far distant. I had often heard before that it might be known by the scent when this animal was near, but had never believed it. We notwithstanding proceeded with our cocked pistols in our hands; the smell soon became as strong as that of castor, and we plainly saw him lying behind some bushes, without appearing to be in the least disturbed by the clang of our cymbals. At our approach he stood up, and seeing him collecting his strength to spring at us, we fired two pistols, neither of which I believe took effect. He then retired with the greatest composure behind some bushes, and disappeared in the wood. Not being at all inclined to attack him without necessity, we took a circuitous course avoid him, and proceeded with as little noise as possible.

It was completely dark when we came to several ruinous and forsaken huts, which, according to our people, formerly belonged to a large village, called *Maderode*, but had been forsaken by the inhabitants on account of the elephants, which had compelled them to leave it.

It sometimes happens that a troop of these animals take a pleasure for a time in visiting such a village in the night, or in passing frequently through it. In that case it is impossible to inhabit the place any longer, not only on account of the continual danger to which the lives of the villagers are exposed, but because they eat up the crops, and even overturn the huts, destroying and crushing to pieces every thing that comes in their way. The people are therefore obliged to abandon the place as soon as possible.

Our quarters were in the middle of a small plain, entirely surrounded with uncommonly large trees. Among the smaller trees that were spread here and there over the plain there was one of considerable size, under which we resolved to pass the night. We therefore collected a large quantity of dry wood, being afraid of a visit from the elephants, which apparently had not yet entirely left this place, as we could observe from the many traces of them around us.

Scarcely had we kindled our fire against the trunk of the tree, and spread our mats, when an innumerable multitude of small green frogs, about the size of beans, fell from the branches, from the heat of the fire, as it were, in showers upon us, and we were under the necessity of removing our quarters to some distance. But we were soon obliged to return to our first position, where the ground was somewhat elevated, as it was here so moist that we could not stand a few minutes on one spot without being wet to the ancles. We therefore returned once more to our tree, and having taken the precaution of previously making a great fire under it, by which the greater part of the remaining frogs were brought down, we made ready our supper, into which, notwithstanding all our care, some of those little animals fell from time to time; but travellers must not be too fastidious.

CHAP. VII.

The lucky shot — Treacherous enemy — Bravery of the Baker — Blood-suckers — Ceylonese Nightingale — Beautiful Wood — Train of Misfortunes --- Dreadful tempest.

On the following day we once more proceeded on our journey, and towards evening arrived off a great sandy plain, without having met with any incident worth relating. We here fixed our quarters by the side of a small brook, filled with weeds and water plants, and bordered, on the side we occupied, with a low but impenetrable hedge of thorns and bushes. A heavy rain, which fell soon after, prevented us from sleeping for the remainder of the night, and we amused ourselves with throwing some of our rockets at the elephants that we plainly saw running away across the plain. At the approach of the fire they speedily took to flight, and the echo of their tremendous roar returned back to us would have been sufficient to fill our souls with dismay, had we not believed ourselves secure behind our fires. We had also, since our departure from *Jaffnapatnam*, began to be in some degree familiar with those animals.

Notwithstanding that we heard from time to time a great noise on the other side of the brook, it gave us very little uneasiness, as the thick hedge I have already mentioned, which traversed the whole plain like a bulwark, rendered us secure from attacks on that side. Towards three o'clock in the morning, this noise increased in an extraordinary degree, and we concluded, from the plashing in the water, and a continual grunting, that a herd of wild swine had come to wallow in the brook.

Though we could see nothing, as it was extremely dark, we, notwithstanding, pointed our muskets in the direction that we supposed them to be, and firing all together, we heard them take to flight with the utmost speed out of the water. Nothing could be more laughable than the confused grunting they set up, in endeavouring to make their escape.

The groans of one of these animals, which we heard after the rest were all gone, made us suppose that it had been wounded, and we waited with impatience for day-break, that we might be convinced of the fact.

As soon as the day began to dawn, we searched on both sides of the brook, but could find nothing. The cooper's slave-boy, however, discovered the animal just as we were about to return, that too much time might not be lost. It lay behind some bushes, to all appearance dead. The baker and myself were the first that arrived, and as there were no signs of life, we did not doubt a moment that we had killed it. The baker therefore took his knife out of his pocket, to cut off its tail, intending to make a present of it, by way of derision, to M. D'Allemand. Smiling with self-complacency, he prepared to execute his purpose, laying hold of the tail with his hand, when the treacherous animal, with a tremendous grunt, suddenly raised himself upon his fore-legs.

The attitude of the baker at this moment was completely picturesque; I cannot even now think of it without laughing; pale as death, he stood fixed to the spot with fear, while I was not altogether without apprehensions for his safety; but seeing that the animal was unable to get up, and had immediately fallen down, we soon recovered ourselves, and the enraged baker, drawing his long sword, plunged it into the animal's side in revenge. Our companions at this moment coming up, were greatly surprised at his fury against the dead swine; but being informed of the adventure, they amused themselves not a little at his expense.

We began immediately to cut up our prize, which was about the size of a tolerably-well fattened European swine, and, with the exception of a few white spots, was almost perfectly black. In its stomach we found pallam, or milk-fruit, and sand. After having cut off the best pieces, we returned to our encampments, and soon again set forward on our journey.

On the way, I had the gratification of seeing a very beautiful ape, entirely white, with a beard of the same colour. Our guide called this also *wandroe*, the name he gave to the black apes we had formerly seen.

On leaving *Jaffnapatnam*, I had imprudently forgotten to provide myself with an additional pair of boots: those I had on were now so completely worn out, that I was obliged to throw them away, and walk barefoot, like the koolies. The stones, holes, and inequalities of the ground, which we often met with on the road, rendered this manner of travelling extremely difficult. But nothing occasioned me so much inconvenience as a sort of thorn, with three points, which were so placed, that one of them was always directed upwards. These thorns are found chiefly in deep, sandy places, but I have never been able to discover the bush or tree that produces them.

We saw a great number of peacocks. I have already mentioned that we had resolved not to shoot any more of these birds, as their flesh is uncommonly hard and dry, and we had our free choice of all the various sorts, and vast multitudes of game and animals with which those woods are filled; as deer, antelopes, hares, partridges, wild fowl, and others of every sort.

Sometime after this we found a nest of bees in the hollow of a tree, which we took possession of, after having expelled the bees by smoke. They were of a very peculiar species, and might have been taken, at first sight, for black flies; their heads, compared with their bodies, appeared to be extremely large; their honey was uncommonly liquid, and had a disagreeable taste. The natives call them *conna*.

Our baker's life was here in great danger, for, carelessly pursuing his way, he happened to tread upon a serpent, which bit him in the calf of his leg, and then crept into the wood. It was fortunate for him that he wore boots; we could see plainly the marks of the teeth, and the venom upon the leather.

At eleven o'clock we came to Conderipo, another solitary hut, or ambelam, situated in the midst of the forest. We hoped to find in it a shelter from the rain, which now fell in great quantities; but when we approached, no one would be the first to enter, afraid that a tiger, or some other wild beast, might have taken up his abode in it. The little light, admitted by the low opening that formed the entrance, was not sufficient to enable us to distinguish objects within. We therefore deemed it advisable to throw in some rockets first, and to hold our arms in readiness;

but the baker, drawing his long sword, and looking at us with a contemptuous smile, called out, that we had only to follow him, and without waiting for our answer went in. Scarcely, however, had he proceeded a few paces in the dark, when we saw him spring back out of the hut in great haste, trembling, and quite pale. We enquired what he had seen; but not being able to answer, he only pointed to a movement in the hut, which we could hear at a short distance, and which seemed to approach the entrance. We therefore resolved to pursue our journey, and rather get wet to the skin, than to engage again in an unnecessary and dangerous combat. But how great was our astonishment, upon seeing a beautiful hound creep out and come towards us. The poor animal, by wagging his tail, seemed to beg some food, which he appeared to be greatly in want of, as he could scarcely stand from weakness and hunger, we supplied him abundantly with victuals, and at two o'clock, left this place; the hound, as will readily be supposed, willingly accompanying us.

We very soon came to a flat, open space, the wet marshy surface of which was covered with plants and weeds; pools, full of muddy stagnant water, were interspersed here and there, in which thick forests of reeds raised their thin tops.

Scarcely had we advanced a few steps in the plain, when an innumerable multitude of bloodsuckers fastened upon us. The koolies and I had our bare legs and feet instantly covered with them, which afforded a subject of mirth to our fellow-travellers, who happened to be better shod. The koolies advised me not to force them off, but to allow them to suck till they were satiated. They were at first about the thickness of a violin-string, and the length of a finger; but when they fell off, being completely filled with blood, we found they had become three times thicker than before.

As soon as we again got into the forest, we put some salt to the mouths of those who still remained upon our feet, when they instantly let go their hold and fell off. Our legs and feet were entirely covered with blood, and though we had crossed the plain in less than a quarter of an hour, I am certain that I lost in that short space of time, at least three ounces of blood. What surprised me most was, how they could possibly fasten themselves upon us so quickly, as we crossed the plain rather running than walking. Their numbers were so incalculably great, that I believe every leaf and blade of grass was loaded with them. During the remainder of our journey, we were several times attacked by these insects, but never in such unheard of multitudes. I have since ascertained that each of them could contain more than half an ounce of blood. These, however, are not so greedy and insatiable as the smaller sort. The inhabitants call them *rettum poetsié.*

In these amazing woods places are sometimes found of great extent, where the ground is free from brambles and underwood, and covered with the most beautiful green. After having passed the marshy plain, we came to a place of this description, where we halted to recover from our fatigue.

The forests of Ceylon have almost always something in them inexpressively great and majestic, that instantly fills the soul with astonishment and admiration.

Trees are there of a prodigious height and thickness, that have outlived several ages, and whose closely-interwoven leaves form an impenetrable shade, and afford a pleasant and refreshing coolness. An incalculable number of birds of every sort are mingled together, and each singing its own natural note, produces a confused but pleasant concert. There are two kinds that far excel all the rest; the one for the beautiful splendour of its feathers, and the other for the melting tones of its voice. The first is the magnificent peacock, whose glowing colours are contrasted with the dark green of these old and venerable woods; the other, a small black bird, about the size of a green-finch, who by its delightful, complaining, and ever-varying notes, inspires a soft and pleasing melancholy. I never grew tired of listening to its melting strains; never have I heard a bird sing so sweetly, and at the same time with so much regularity or science, if I may be allowed the expression. The so much admired nightingale is not to be at all compared with this unknown songster of the lonely wilderness.

How beautiful is nature when she shows herself in all her simplicity, and without the misplaced additions and changes of art. She has then something attractive, something so perfectly congenial to the original state of our senses and our soul, that I have often felt an irresistible desire to spend my days in these terrestrial paradises—the forests of Ceylon.

I have travelled in many forests, and traversed many woods in various countries; but never have I seen one that could, in any degree, be compared to those of Ceylon. There, when the sun shoots his burning rays, only a trembling and coloured light can be perceived. Trees, almost as old as the world, spread a refreshing coolness, and proudly exalting themselves on high, extend their branches far and wide into the air. Others, loaded with wild fruit, protect aromatic plants that grow in their shade, and fill the atmosphere with a balmy and refreshing fragrance. Butterflies, of the most splendid and glowing colours, wander among the trembling leaves, or pursue one another in sport. Here and there are seen through the trees, as in perspective, troops of deer, elks, and antelopes of all sorts, and sometimes bears and wild swine. Game swarms on all sides; hares, partridges, wild fowl; while the cooing of pigeons, and other birds of that species, continually resounds through the forest. Apes of various sorts skip from branch to branch, and have often afforded us much amusement, by a thousand ridiculous leaps and grimaces. In short, these enchanting forests had, for me, so many attractions, that whenever I recal them to mind, I feel an irresistible longing to see them again. How passionately I desire to wander once more under their delightful shades, and again to listen to the sweet and melodious voices of the plumed inhabitants. But to return to our journey.

We came, then, in a short time, to another opening, or free space in the wood, but much larger than the former; it was, properly speaking, a lake, or large morass, the water of which had been dried up by the sun. Three or four days later we might have passed through it with dry feet, but now, when we tried to get over, we sank almost to the knees in black sticky mud, which obliged us to make a large circle. We here saw many hoof marks of elephants, buffaloes, and wild swine.

The day began to decline as we arrived at the other side of the marsh. Notwithstanding the unwholesome smell that arose from it, and the want of water, we should have passed the night here, but our guide persuaded us to continue our march, by promising to bring us to a spring of excellent water, which, according to his account, could not be more than a mile distant at farthest.

A great dispute instantly commenced between him and the Koolies, who insisted he was going to take the wrong path. But as we placed more confidence in him than the others, we brought the dispute to an end by declaring that we should follow the guide. We had, however, cause to repent of our partiality; for, after having wandered during upwards of three hours, now to the right, and then to the left hand, without being able to find the desired place, I could observe, by the anxious appearance of our guide, that he had lost his way, though he kept continually assuring us that we were near the place of our destination. At last he acknowledged that he did not know where he was, which immediately drew a whole torrent of abuse upon him from the Koolies.

We at last came to a small river, the banks of which were very steep. As the side on which we were was poorly provided with trees, and the forest on the opposite bank appeared to be thick and close, we resolved, in order to protect ourselves from the rain which still continued to fall, to take up our quarters there, and pass the river by fording. But our guide informed us that it was deep, and very dangerous to cross in the dark, not only from the pits in the channel, but on account of the crocodiles, of which it was full, we soon changed our resolution, and prepared for passing the night where we were.

It was now late, it rained, and we durst not separate far from one another, to search for dry wood. We found on the spot scarcely as much as served to keep up a small fire during the night, which gave us considerable uneasiness. Our tranquillity was not increased by the noise and cracking heard at a distance, and the frequent traces of elephants we had met with during the day, from which we concluded that those animals were in great numbers in this part of the forest.

When it became necessary to bring water for preparing our supper, the Koolies were so terrified at the idea of being attacked by the crocodiles, that they with one voice refused to approach the river, though we offered to accompany them with torches and our pistols in our hands. What surprized us most was, that their obstinate and determined refusal inspired us with the same terror, so that instead of a supper, we were under the necessity of contenting ourselves with a glass of liquor and some biscuits.

The rain decreased in some measure, but the thick clouds with which the heavens were overcast, produced an awful darkness, and gave the signal of an approaching tempest. The thunder now began to roll, the flashes of lightning followed in rapid succession, and very soon the whole firmament seemed to be in an entire blaze. The suffocating and oppressive atmosphere rendered our breathing difficult, and not the least agitation of the air refreshed our languid bodies. A deep silence prevailed in this wilderness, interrupted only now and then by the dreadful claps of the thunder; no wild beast was heard. Scarcely were our eyes blinded by the quick flashes of the lightning than we found ourselves suddenly placed in the midst of thick and impenetrable darkness. Although accustomed to similar eruptions of nature, which are very common in those countries, yet we could not prevent a sort of anxiety, a kind of disagreeable sensation, from overcoming our minds. Perhaps the situation in which we were placed contributed in a great degree to produce this feeling.

Our Koolies alone seemed to be quite indifferent; and without showing the least signs of terror at this awful noise, they amused themselves with smoking and singing; some of them even slept in the greatest tranquillity.

At last the atmosphere discharged itself in a heavy rain, which extinguished our fire. Without any other roof than the sky, we had crept together under our talpats which, however, did not prevent us from being wet to the skin. As it was impossible to kindle our fire again, we lighted some of our torches; and having planted half a dozen of them round us, we each held a couple in our hands, ready to throw at the first enemy that should dare to approach us.

About three o'clock in the morning the rain ceased entirely; we still heard the thunder rolling, but at a great distance, and with a feeble and expiring noise. But now the wild beasts made their appearance, which, during the storm, had concealed themselves in their holes and dens. We often observed them at a distance, where it is probable the banks of the river were less steep, and afforded them an easier passage than the place where we had, fortunately for us, taken up our quarters.

As we did not consider our torches sufficient to protect us from the attacks of wild beasts, we threw a rocket from time to time, into the thick darkness that surrounded us; for, no sooner had the rain ceased, than our ears rung with the croaking of frogs, and the stunning buz of thousands of insects, particularly a sort of cricket, whose shrill and penetrating cry rose out of every bush, and we had great difficulty to hear one another speak, and still less to notice the approach of wild beasts.

Wet through and through, and worn out with hunger, and want of sleep, we waited impatiently for the dawn of day, which at last, to our great joy, made its appearance.

CHAPTER VIII.

Crocodiles—Dangerous passage—The Oedoembo—The Friendly Asiaulic—Golgom—" Polonga! Polonga!"—Postlan—Madompe—Arrival at Chilaw—Mr. Van der Weiden—Chilaw—The Wedding—Departure.

As soon as objects could be distinguished, we put our stiff and benumbed limbs in motion, and while we and some of the koolies collected a considerable quantity of dry wood, M. D'Allemand and the cooper went into the forest, and, in a short time, returned with a hare and two partridges.

We now found that the koolies had told us the truth respecting the crocodiles, as we saw several amphibious animals swimming here and there in the river, and even lying on the banks, on the opposite side; they appeared to me to be smaller than those I had seen at Batavia and other places. As our people had exhibited so much terror at the crocodiles, we were curious to see how they would conduct themselves in passing the river. The instant we had finished our breakfast, and while the baggage was getting ready, one of them took the half of a cocoa-nut, into which he let fall several drops of his blood. After having mixed this with water, and the oil of *sinsjelie*, or *sesame*,* and in a low voice repeated his charm, or conjuration over it, he annointed the foreheads of all his companions with it. But all his endeavours to induce us to undergo the same operation were in vain, though he insisted that there was no other way of passing the river without danger, than by using this *pilisuniam*, or charm, by which he had shut the jaws of the crocodiles. We, however, resisted all his entreaties, because we considered this superstitious ceremony as wholly useless, and altogether without effect upon the jaws of the ravenous monsters; and were beginning to consider of some other way of getting over, when the koolie who had performed the ceremony addressed me as follows:—

"Aya, (Sir) you are mistaken in not putting confidence in the charm that I have just been repeating; do you then believe, that we should dare to expose ourselves to be devoured by the crocodiles, if we were not certain of the infallibility of my art? In order to convince you of this, I shall, at the head of half the koolies, go over to the other side of the river, and return alone, to bring you and the rest over; you will then be able to judge for yourself, if the passage be accompanied with as much danger as you believe: and you have certainly more courage than my comrades."

This well-timed piece of flattery, which excited our self-love, accomplished what nothing else could do; we agreed to his proposal, curious to know how he would acquit himself in the affair.

Five of them taking the baggage on their heads, set out for the other side of the river. After having muttered some words to himself, which we did not understand, he put a considerable quantity of sand into his mixture, and made as many small round balls of it as there were persons in our company. Having thrown six of these into the water, they forded the river without showing the least appearance of uneasiness, and reached the opposite bank in safety. Our conjurer now threw only one of his bullets into the water, and came back with the same good fortune, without the crocodiles making the least motion of attacking him, though we could plainly see the snouts above the water, of several that were swimming here and there, not ten yards distant from him. We at last decided to venture the passage, and having informed our leader, he made us place our left hands upon each others shoulders, and threw the remaining little balls into the water; he, at the same time, conjured us not to change our position, saying, that as we would not consent to have the sign put upon us, the only means of avoiding misfortunes was, not to

* A plant, the fruit of which contains a number of oblong seeds, from which an oil is extracted that is very useful for burning, and other purposes, but especially for strengthening the nerves.

lose our hold of one another, otherwise he could not answer for any accidents that might happen. Then, taking the dog under his arm, and holding by the hand the baker, who had placed himself at the head of this resolute band, we followed him with the rest of the koolies, into the water, with our hunting-knives in our hands by way of precaution. This, however, was unnecessary, as the crocodiles did not seem to observe, or, at least, they paid no attention to us, and without any accident we reached the opposite bank.

We were no sooner upon dry land, than our companions made ready their guns to attack a crocodile that was lying asleep on the sand, about fifty yards from us; but all the koolies joining together, begged them not to molest the animal, otherwise, as they said, their comrade, who had prepared the *pilisunium*, would certainly meet with some misfortune. I also advised them against it, not deeming it prudent to disturb or irritate him without cause. The cooper, however, not willing that his gun should have been loaded for nothing, shot an *ædoembo*, a sort of lizard of an extraordinary large size, that was creeping among the rocks in the river.

This animal, which is called in the Cingalese language *teelgoin*, differs in nothing from the crocodile, except its size; it is of a greyish colour on the back, which changes to a yellow on the belly. It incessantly shakes its blue-forked tongue, and blows with its jaws widely extended; it uses its long slender tail as a whip for its defence; fish is its principal food, and certainly also, grass and vegetables, as we found both in the stomach of the one we killed. The length of it from the head to the point of the tail, was full two feet and a half. They are not usually of such large dimensions; measuring only from eighteen inches to two feet at most. As this animal is found in every part of India, it is unnecessary to give any further description of it; I shall only mention a few particulars that seem to have escaped the notice of other travellers.

Its flesh is considered as a remedy for disorders of the stomach. The Indians even insist, that the weakest person is able to digest it, and that those who can bear no other food upon their stomachs, retain this perfectly well. I know from experience, that it has one extremely invigorating property. In order to prepare it for use, the head, the feet, and the tail, are thrown away, and the skin is taken off. The flesh is then cut into small pieces, and a *cassaia*, or decoction made of it, which, when allowed to cool, forms itself into a gluey consistence, like a decoction of hartshorn, and of an equally strengthening quality. The flesh dissolves very easily; its taste is like fish, but not disagreeable: one must, however, be accustomed to it, to overcome the aversion excited by the hideous form of the animal.

It was nine o'clock before we reached the opposite bank of this little river. Contrary to our expectations the weather cleared up, and the thick vapours, with which the air was loaded, having dispersed by degrees, the sun again appeared in all his splendour in the azure vault of heaven. Thousands of the winged inhabitants of the ever-blooming woods offered their accustomed morning's salution, and dried their moistened feathers in his cherishing beams. As the rain had not used us much better than them, we followed their example, and having strengthened ourselves with a good draught of rum, we resumed our journey with renewed courage and vigour.

At one o'clock in the afternoon we crossed a river called *Ambolonga*, by means of a large tree felled on purpose, the roots of which served us for a bridge. When we had reached the other side, I found there the thickest tree I had ever seen; eighteen men would have with difficulty been able to measure the circumference with their arms extended; and its branches swarmed with multitudes of birds of every sort, red apes, and squirrels. We soon after entered a delightful grove, where we found a party of *Cingalese*, consisting of twenty-three persons, with seventeen oxen. We lay down not far from them, and when we had finished our dinner, I approached and enquired, in the Malabar language, if any person among them could speak it. An aged man then sat up and answered me in broken Malabar: he made me sit down by him upon a mat that was spread on the ground, offered me betel and cegars, and we entered in conversation upon various subjects. Among other things I put many questions to him respecting Conde-udda, the interior of the country, and the manner in which the Emperor treated Europeans who fell into his hands, whether by desertion, treachery, or otherwise. The good old man readily answered all my enquiries, and informed me that when he left *Colombo*, two Dutch ambassadors had just returned from Candy, the Emperor's capital, where they were treated with great distinction, and had been presented with two large elephants by the emperor; who had at the same time abolished the customs, according to which the ambassadors were formerly obliged to approach the throne kneeling, with the company's letter upon their heads; besides other humiliating ceremonies. He further informed me, that he himself was called *Manioppoe*, and that he was *axiaulic* or caterer to the emperor in the Province of *Colilwilla*. He had been at Colombo, where he had sold arrack, tobacco, cardamoms, &c. The two oxen covered with white linen, were loaded with various articles for the emperor's table, and the rest belonged to himself. I made known to him my desire of exploring the interior of the country, and particularly to visit the metropolis of Candy. He replied that this depended entirely upon myself; the Mestese had nothing to fear, as they could travel all over the country with a passport. He advised me, however, if my journey had no other object than curiosity, not to venture to Candy itself, as I might be suspected of having some evil intention, which could not fail of bringing me into perplexity and danger.

I could not forbear laughing to myself when the good old man took me for a Mestese.—It is true I had altogether the manner and exterior appearance of one, and he was only in part deceived, for besides being without shoes or stockings, my face was quite sunburnt, and I spoke the Malabar language very fluently. When we were about to depart, he told me that if ever my way should lie through his village, (which he named) I had only to enquire for him, when I might rest assured of receiving all the service from him that lay in his power. In conclusion, he presented me with some white hunter's cakes made of sugar of the country, besides something like sweatmeat, which he called *ogullai*, of a delicious taste. I gave him, in return, the pencil with which I had taken down in my pocket-book the name of his village, as he appeared very desirous of possessing it. I then took leave of this worthy old man, not knowing that I should one day, next to God, have him to thank for my life. An instant after they set out, and as they passed by us, my friend put his hand to his head, and said very kindly, *Salams, aya! nella yoquem!* Farewell, sir, I wish you much happiness! I observed that they had with them three Lascars, or Indian soldiers, armed with matchlocks, the others were provided with darts and bows and arrows.

We regretted extremely our not having brought fishing tackle with us from Jaffnapatnam, we should otherwise have been in no want of fish, for the rivers, particularly that on the banks of which we had halted, swarmed with every sort; even the half-dried pools and marshes were full of them.

At three o'clock we again set forward, passing sometimes through delightful groves composed of high and large trees, resounding with the songs and voices of an unspeakable number of birds, among which the green turtle-dove was delightfully melodious: our way at other times lay through sandy plains covered with high and close underwood. It was about four o'clock when we heard the sound of human voices, and soon after we entered a poor village, consisting of about a dozen wretched huts. This place was called *Golgom*, and the inhabitants spoke nothing but the Cingalese language:—we found, however, provisions, such as milk, eggs, and cocoa-nuts, very cheap and in abundance. Though the people showed us a large empty hut for the accommodation of travellers passing that way, we preferred to sit down as usual in the open air, under the trees. Towards evening, however, we repaired to the hut, that we might be secure from the attacks of wild beasts, where we passed a tolerably quiet night.

The next day soon after our departure, we entered a narrow crooked path, which led us through the middle of a beautiful wood; about ten o'clock this path turned suddenly to the right, and soon after we found ourselves in a large sandy plain, from which, to our great joy, we discovered the sea, and the village of *Poetlan*, on the shore, at a considerable distance; but before we reached it, an end was nearly put to my life and journey together, by the following occurrence.

Not far from the village I found some boys busy with sticks at the trunk of a decayed hollow tree. Upon coming up to them I perceived that a serpent had crept into the hollow: having always had a great aversion to that dangerous tribe, I chopped off with my cutlass a piece of its tail, that was still hanging out of the hole by which it had crept in; stooping down at the same time to see where it had gone, it appeared at another opening above me, and at the instant when it was ready to dart at my head, (which I had uncovered that I might see the better,) the boys all called out together—*Polanga! Polanga!*—and at the same time drawing me back by my clothes, they saved me from almost certain death, for the bite of the *Polanga* (as I have said in my general description of the animals of Ceylon,) is fatal.

Having cut this dangerous enemy in pieces, I joined my companions, who had left me far behind them, and we reached, about ten o'clock, the dwelling of the commandant of *Poetlan*, whose name was *Bodenschatz*; he was then on business at Colombo, but his serjeant, *Tournoi*, who commanded in his absence, received us with great civility. He was extremely surprised to see the dog we had found by the way, and which had always followed us since, and informed us that it was one of the favourite hounds of his master, who had lost it about three weeks before on a hunting party. We could not comprehend how this poor animal had wandered so long and so far without having been devoured by a tiger; and how he had got food during all that time was completely a riddle to us.

We resolved to remain here for some days, to recover from the fatigues of our journey, but M. D'Allemand, being in too much haste, hired an andol and set out next day for Colombo.

Poetlan is situated on the shore of the straits of *Calpentin*, opposite to the island of the same name. It is a large and very populous village, but the environs are far from being agreeable. There is here a small fort with four bastions, still in tolerably good repair, but quite forsaken and miserable; the garrison, consisting of fifty soldiers, chiefly Topazes and Lascars, live in the village.

They build at *Poetlan*, sloops, tunnies, and other small Indian vessels, in which the trade is carried on from the straits of Calpentin along the whole coasts of the island. There is also at this place one of the three principal salt works in Ceylon; the two others are at *Baticalao** and *Learawa*;† they are all in the possession of the Dutch, who have the whole coast of the island in their power.

For some time our way lay through a barren and sandy district; but after an hour's walk it became considerably better, and more fertile. About nine o'clock we came to a pond full of muddy water, where we had nearly caught a porcupine, but, though wounded, it escaped among the thickets. A Topaze, who had joined us at *Poetlan*, that he might have the advantage of our company as far as Chilaw, advised us to follow the sea-shore, where we should find villages and provisions in abundance; but our guide, and the koolies, who suffered extremely from the heat, and the deep rough sand, persuaded us to approach nearer to the forest, which lay about half a mile to the left, where we should be protected both from the sun and rain. We agreed to this proposal, and soon entered the forest, which, however, did not answer either our or the koolies' expectations. They had, it is true, no longer to struggle with the deep sand, but, on the other hand, they found it more difficult to get through the bushes and thorns, which surrounded the trees, and wounded their naked limbs in a dreadful manner. The first object we saw was a troop of wild swine, from which the cooper inferred that we should soon have good sport; and he was not deceived, for a short time after we killed a deer. We took our dinner on the banks of a rivulet, which was almost dry, and the bed full of rocks and stones, among which we saw here and there small red fishes swimming.

After resting two hours, we again set out, and soon after observed among the trees an uncommonly large elephant, amusing himself by plucking small branches from the trees, which he ate, after having shaken and struck them against his sides, to clear them of the insects with which they were covered. It is probable that he observed us, as he turned his head towards the spot where we were, and shook his broad ears, but he allowed us to pass without molestation.

At the close of the day we came to a small plain, encircled with high trees. We found here some huts, forming a village,

---

* *Baticalao*, a Province in the eastern part of the island.

† *Learawa*. The district, or county of Learawa, lies to the east of *Ceylon*, in the Province of *Jalé*.

called *Medampe.* As the inhabitants could speak nothing but Cingalese, one of our koolies served as interpreter. He made them provide some dried fish and flesh, besides some *tinné*, a sort of meal, and, as the weather appeared cloudy, we slept in one of the huts, which they gave up to us for a small acknowledgment. These people were obliged to keep up several large fires at night, not far from their habitations, and to watch by turns, in order to drive away the elephants, which were in the neighbouring forest, and very frequently visited this little open plain. We heard their hideous cries and shouts, which the echo returned in the stilness of the night, resounding through the solitary woods.

Early the next morning we once more set forward. The wood through which we passed was abundantly provided with wild fruit, particularly with one kind, that our koolies called *dang*, about the size of a plum, of a black colour, and a pleasant though bitter taste. There was another, called *pergodhi*, a sort of very sweet apple, with three stones, or kernels. We also found, to my great surprise, several *Moronga-trees*. This tree has an uncommonly rough bark, and a blue dye stuff is extracted from the wood. The fruit is about a foot long, round and green, and of the appearance and thickness of asparagus, with a bulb at the extremity; it is eaten boiled like vegetables. The Dutch call it *Drum-sticks*, from its shape. It is probable that the seed of this tree had been carried into the wood by the wind, or by birds, as it is very seldom to be found in uninhabited places.

The ground was here extremely uneven, full of rocks and sharp stones, probably on account of its vicinity to the mountains. I had fortunately purchased a pair of shoes from the Commandant at Poetlan, otherwise I could not have proceeded without much pain and difficulty. The wood now became somewhat more open, and less overgrown with thickets and brambles. We found from time time, in our way, small plains, and marshes half dried up, the surface of which was sometimes not sufficiently strong to prevent us from sinking up to the knees, when we ventured to cross them. Towards the evening we halted in the middle of a small grove, under a large tree, with very thick foliage, in the branches of which an innumerable multitude of small birds had taken up their abode for the night: the confused noise of their songs had nearly deafened us, before they became quiet. When the fire was kindled, we amused ourselves with drinking and smoking till supper was prepared; after which, notwithstanding the continual distant sound of the elephants, which was heard during the whole night, we slept quietly till day-break, when we again commenced our journey.

It was near eleven o'clock in the morning, when we reached the river Chilaw, which is very deep, broad, and rapid. It was not till we had shouted repeatedly with all our might, that we were heard on the opposite shore. At last, we observed two men step into a vessel kept there for the accommodation of travellers, and row towards us; we availed ourselves of the interval to change our linen and clothes, that we might make a decent appearance before the commandant of the place.

As soon as we arrived at the town, we presented ourselves to him. He received us with great kindness, and offered the church, or a hall, used for the same purpose, which formed part of his house, for our accommodation, as well as his table, as long as we chose to remain. His name was Van der Weiden; he was brother to the captain of an East India ship with whom I had formerly been intimate, having lived in the same house with him at the Cape of Good Hope, where he was afterwards unfortunately killed by an English captain. He was the kindest man that can well be imagined; he entertained us with the best of every thing he had, though we were not official travellers, and had nothing to distinguish us in our dress or appearance. He informed us that M. D'Allemand had passed through the place two days before our arrival, and in such extreme haste to reach Colombo, that it was with difficulty he could be persuaded to dine with him.

The next day, when we were going to set out, he pressed us so strongly to stay a few days with him, that it was impossible for us to refuse. It cost us, no doubt, more *batta*, or provision for our koolies, but, on the other hand, we recovered from our fatigue, and were served and entertained like kings. The commandant's secretary, a very worthy man, had the goodness to conduct us through the place, and show us every thing worthy of notice that it contained.

Chilaw is a large village, very pleasantly situated in a grove of cocoa-trees. The river, from which the place takes its name, and on whose banks it is situated, separates it from the shore of the sea, from which it is about a mile distant. This river takes its rise among the mountains of Bocaul, and flows, as has been just observed, past Chilaw into the sea. There is here an old fort, small, and of a square form; it was built by the Portuguese, the first conquerors of India, and has since been repaired and improved. In time of peace, the garrison consists of from thirty to fifty men, chiefly Topazes and Lascars, but on account of the war with the English, it has been reinforced with two hundred Europeans and Malays, which, from the strong situation of the place, was a force more than sufficient to defend it against an enemy twenty times more numerous. As it is surrounded on almost every side by frightful wildernesses, and can only be approached in boats by the river, which is broad and rapid, it runs no danger whatever of being taken by surprise, if the usual watch is kept; and besides, the guns of the fort command the banks of the river, and can prevent its being approached.

On the last night of our stay here we were invited to a wedding, to which we were conducted by the secretary of the commandant. We entered a large straw hut, illuminated by a multitude of wax tapers, where we found a number of women and girls seated on chairs and benches, placed along the walls of the hut, which were hung with white linen. The apartment not being sufficiently large for so many people, the men were obliged to remain without, under the cocoa-trees, where they amused themselves with drinking fresh *surie*, and smoking cegars; but no sooner had they learnt that we were strangers, than we were invited to go into the hut. Every one treated us with the greatest kindness and distinction, and overloaded us with civilities.

Among the various sorts of cakes and sweetmeats, which were presented to us in great abundance, there was one of the last-mentioned kind, of an excellent and peculiarly agreeable taste. The women eat with their tea a sort of dried fish, or elk-flesh well salted and peppered. The Mestese females, as well as the Portuguese, in Ceylon and the coast, generally prefer any thing salted, to sugar or sweetmeats, to use with their tea.

As soon as supper was ready, a table was erected the whole length of the hut, composed of boards placed upon empty casks, and covered with white linen. This was soon loaded with a multitude of dishes full of rice, curry, and many other compositions, all extremely well prepared. Every guest first served his lady with what she chose, after which he filled his own plate; and all were emptied without the assistance of spoons or forks, the hand and fingers being, according to the custom of the country, used instead of them. Our drink consisted of punch, arrack, and *vellipatty*. No sooner was supper over than preparations were made for dancing, by taking away the table, and making the hut clear of incumbrances. The musicians next made their appearance, with their gomgoms (drums of an immense size,) three violins, and a sort of flute; but the hut having no floor, we were obliged to dance in the sand, and I was almost suffocated by the clouds of dust which rose around us. The dancing continued, however, without interruption,—fandangos, quadrilles, and Cingalese dances, which last consist of sundry strange leaps and twists of the body, and followed in rapid succession. The baker, who had entered keenly into the sport, far excelled all the rest in the Cingalese style, and kept the whole company, but particularly the female part of it, in a continual roar of laughter, at his ridiculous grimaces and attitudes.

At midnight, the new married couple repaired to another hut, and the dancing, drinking, and singing, continued with equal spirit till day-break, when our koolies (according to the orders they had received) came to inform us, to the infinite regret of the baker, that it was time to depart. Several of the company endeavoured to persuade us to stay a day or two with them, or at least to remain in the village, but we were obliged to refuse, mentioning, among other reasons, that we had the night before taken leave of the commandant, upon which they all offered us the use of their houses and tables. But having thanked these good people for their generous and hospital offer, we took farewell of the whole company, and soon after recommenced our journey.

CHAPTER IX.

Ambelam of Marawille—The generous enemy—Specimen of the Cingalese language—The friendly priest—Unsuccessful enterprize of the Dutch against the emperor of Condé Udda—Negombo—The fallen cocoa-nuts—Country-house of governor Hock—*The cooper's life in danger—Arrival at* Colombo.

Our path now lay along a kind of dyke, from which we could discover the sea on our right, and on our left the immeasurable and savage forest of *Medampe*;—in several places we observed traces of tigers and serpents.

About five o'clock we came to *Marawille*, a large village situated in an agreeable plain, almost half a mile from the sea: great numbers of cattle were grazing around the village. The majoral conducted us to some distance from the place, to a grove of cocoa-trees, where the ambelam or resting place was situated.

We supped near a large fire we had kindled a few paces from the ambelam; after which we entered this place of rest, as it was called, that we might be protected from the rain, which had begun to fall, as well as from the attacks of wild beasts. Our koolies lay round the fire in the best manner they were able.

The ambelam was situated on the side of a broad canal or ditch, half dried up, full of bushes, and such an innumerable multitude of frogs that we were almost deafened with their croaking. This canal was the only separation between us and the savage and far-extended wilderness of *Medampe*, in which were heard the unceasing roar of ravenous beasts.

When my companions had resigned themselves to sleep, I opened a window, or rather hole covered with leaves of a palm-tree, which looked towards the desert of Medampé. The darkness prevented me from seeing any thing but the fire-flies, which were no doubt attracted by the stagnant water of the canal; they danced round the bushes in confused and ever-changing circles. In this immeasurable and dreary plain, an infinite number of savage animals had their abode, especially wild buffaloes, those mighty and untameable cattle that know no master, and never bend their necks to the yoke.

The rain ceased at last, and as there was so little room in the hut, that we could not lie down, but were obliged to sit on the benches, we placed ourselves among the koolies by the fire, and very soon a deep sleep overcame our wearied limbs.

About day break I was suddenly awoke by the outcries of our people. On opening my eyes, I saw with terror two immensely large elephants, not ten yards from us, very quietly plucking the branches from the trees for food. Fortunately one of our koolies was awoke by the noise they made, otherwise we should have ran great danger of being crushed under their feet, as our watch had fallen asleep, and the fire was gone out.

They were so terrified by the sudden shout we gave, and the fire of our guns, that they instantly took to flight,—but how great was our astonishment and terror when we saw them return a few seconds after. They came at a full trot, giving at the same time a terrible roar, while we were scarcely recovered from our first terror. In a moment we were soon dispersed as if blown away by the wind. One ran here, and another there, afraid of being pursued, leaving our guns and baggage a prey to the enemy, which, however, was more generous than we expected; for after having put us to flight, they slowly and with the greatest tranquillity left the grove, only now and then breaking a bough from the trees, and roaring from time to time.

As soon as we supposed they had departed, we came out of our hiding places, and as the day had begun to dawn, we broke up and pursued our journey. We now kept by the sea-shore at the distance of a quarter of a mile, and very soon fell in with a watch-hut, where we found three Lascars, or Indian soldiers, known on the coast by the name of Sepoys. These people informed us that they had been stationed there to give the alarm when any English ships approached the shore with the design of attempting to land, either for the purpose of plundering and destroying the surrounding countries, or of any other hostile intention. They showed us a large pile of wood, to which they were to set fire on such an event taking place, to alarm the other posts, which were placed at certain distances along the whole coast, and in this manner to convey the intelligence to the towns and forts.

At two o'clock we crossed the river *Caimella* in a boat; this river takes its rise in the mountains *Attegall*, and flows into the sea at this place. On the opposite bank is situated the agreeable village of *Gamiepallie.* As we were much pleased with this place, and provisions, particularly fish, were in great abundance, we sat down to dinner under a large Talpat-tree, the ambelam, like all the others in Ceylon, being small, dirty, and dark. The fish we found here was excellent, and we, as well as our Koolies, made a hearty meal.

From the time of our departure from *Poetlan,* the first place where Cingalese only was spoken, I had begun to write down a great number of the words of that language, that I might make use of them in time of need. I found it to be a mixture of the *Grindamee, Hindostanee,* and *Malabar* or *Tamul,* languages ; as the reader may find by the following words :

English.	*Cingalese.*	*Hindostanee.*
Rice.	Haul.	Chaul.
Boiled Rice.	Bat.	Bhat.
Village.	Gom.	Gram.
Tree.	Ghah.	Ghash.
Pepper.	Miris.	Miris.
One.	Eckhoi.	Eck.
Three.	Tenoi.	Tiin.
Five.	Panchoi.	Paneh.
Leaf.	Pat.	Paat.

Besides a great number of words which have a similar resemblance.

The next day, at four o'clock, we left this village, directing our course through a most beautiful district, interspersed with delightful groves of cocoa-trees, and pleasantly situated villages, in one of which, called *Toptoore,* we passed the night. The inhabitants of this place were of the Roman Catholic religion, and had a church and priest. These black christians, as may well be supposed, are very good catholics, being chiefly the offspring of those converts which the Portuguese made with the knife at their throats. There are many villages under the Dutch where this religion is professed, particularly in the neighbourhood of *Colombo* and *Julés ;* but more to the north, and chiefly in the kingdom of *Jaffnapatnam,* most of the black christians are protestants of the Dutch church.

These christians, as they are called, whether catholics or protestants, know nothing of christianity but the name, and are all, so far as religion is concerned, plunged in the deepest ignorance. With the former it is enough to make the sign of the cross, and to carry it round their necks of copper or gold ; for the other it is sufficient to mutter a prayer. With regard to the *Gentoos,* or Pagans, that live under the Dutch government in Ceylon, they are allowed the free exercise of their religion, but are not permitted to have temples, or to make processions of idols, or other religious ceremonies of a similar kind.

The priest of this village having learned that several European travellers from *Jaffnapatnam* were arrived, sent his beadle to request us to sup with him, and to take up our abode at his house. This happened very opportunely, as the ambelam was small, dirty, and full of travellers, and we had already prepared to pass the night in the open air, under the cocoa-trees, when we received his invitation. We therefore repaired without delay to the habitation of the good monk, who received us with unfeigned hospitality, and entertained us with an excellent supper and punch, which is the usual drink of Europeans of the middle class, wine being too expensive.

Our host was of the order of St. Francis, a man of a robust constitution, and about forty years old, nearly the half of which he had passed in Ceylon. He was a Frenchman, a native of *Dijon*; and his joy was excessive when he learned that I spoke his mother tongue, which he had in a great measure forgotten, at least he could not express himself with ease and fluency in it. We entertained each other till after midnight, my companions having gone early to bed. He gave me an account of his life, in which, however, there was nothing very particular, except that he had been present during the expensive and unfortunate war that the Dutch East India Company had carried on against the emperor of Candy, and which, though they took possession of his capital, ended most fatally for them. The circumstances that occasioned this unfortunate and destructive war were as follow.

Soon after the arrival of M. *Schroder*, as governor of the island of Ceylon, he formed the design of extending the cultivation of cinnamon, which then grew only in the emperor's dominions, to the lands belonging to the Dutch East India Company. This plan was formed for the purpose of relieving the company from being always under the necessity of requesting liberty of the emperor to take the bark from the cinnamon trees which request was always as a matter of course accompanied with costly presents. He sent his plan to Batavia, where being greatly approved of by the council, he was invested with full powers to act to the best of his judgment in accomplishing the object of it.

The land on which it was supposed the cinnamon-tree would thrive best, was the property of the people, and possessed and inhabited by them. Without regarding the want and misery that must of necessity have overwhelmed those wretched beings, if robbed of their lands, upon the produce of which they existed, the governor ordered them to give up their land to the company, and remove to a barren waste district, which was appointed for them, and where they might settle if they chose. These poor people not being able to consent with indifference to leave the houses and gardens, and the fields they had cultivated, all their lawful property, made many ineffectual remonstrances, and sent many petitions in vain. Finding that their requests met with no attention, and that preparations were making to expel them by force from their possessions, they petitioned the Emperor of *Candy* for his protection and interference. The emperor instantly dispatched an ambassador to the governor, requesting him to consider that the land possessed by those people legally belonged to them, and that if the company were resolved upon taking it from them, they ought at least to give them as fertile land in exchange for it, that they might not suffer by the losses they would incur by abandoning their habitations, fields, and possessions.

The haughty governor treated the ambassador with contempt, and having sent him back to his master with an insulting answer, took possession by force of the lands of these unfortunate people. It will readily be supposed that the emperor could not allow this affront to pass unrevenged; he therefore immediately after declared war against the Dutch, and the whole island rose in arms to oppose them.

An army of five thousand men was now sent against the emperor to attack him in his own impenetrable forests. But, as may well be imagined, this was no easy undertaking, of which many tragical examples have been furnished by the Portuguese, in the complete destruction of their armies; the expeditions of *Constantinus de Sa, Ludovicus Tissera,* and others may be mentioned as instances.

The Hollanders had no sooner arrived in the midst of the forest than they found themselves as it were surrounded with great trees, which the *Cingalese* had cut down during the night to prevent their march; and while the troops were occupied in clearing their way, the natives, concealed behind the trees, and in the thick foliage of the branches, spread death all around; while none could tell whence the fatal dart was aimed. The priest remarked that they particularly selected the officers and drummers as objects, and the flights of arrows were chiefly directed against them, so that at last nobody would beat the march, and the officers were obliged to dress themselves in the uniform of the privates, that they might not be so easily recognized. The waggons with the ammunition and provisions, met with the same obstacles; for, as the route behind the army was rendered impassable by the Cingalese, it was equally difficult for the baggage and the escort to come up with the army, as it was for the army to advance; they ran the same danger from the deadly arrows of the Cingalese, and frequently during the night, trees of immense thickness and height, which had been previously nearly sawn through, fell upon them, crushing to the earth men, beasts, and baggage waggons. In the mean time the whole of the army were night and day full of anxiety and continually on the watch.—All the wells and ponds on their route were poisoned, so that being heated by the march and the difficulties they had to struggle with, they greedily swallowed the fatal draught and fell by hundreds together.

In a word, they found themselves at last obliged to make a shameful retreat with much difficulty and loss, and to flee before an enemy they had not even seen. The undertaking was once more attempted, but with as little success, and with the same loss. The governor *Schroder* was however promoted to be a member of the council at *Batavia*, and soon after departed to take upon him the functions of that office.

Baron *Van Ech*, the new governor, at last succeeded, though not before he had made many fruitless attempts, in penetrating through the country and savage woods, along the beaten paths and passes of the mountains, which were treacherously left open to him by one of the emperor's generals. In a short time his arms reached the river *Mawveliegonga*, which surrounds Candy, the chief city, on three sides, and pitched his camp on its banks. The emperor having early intelligence of this had sent his women and treasures to the impassable mountains which rise behind his capital, and entered into a negotiation for peace. But the Dutch, grown presumptuous by success, thought of nothing less than making the emperor himself their prisoner, and rejected all the proposals he made to them. They therefore passed the river and made themselves masters of the city without the least opposition, for the place was abandoned and almost empty. All that was found remaining was plundered, and the temples and palaces destroyed; in short, they overloaded themselves with booty, and did not open their eyes to their situation, till they were surrounded and shut up by thousands of Cingalese, who intercepted, and cut off all the supplies and reinforcements sent them from Colombo. Famine soon began to be felt among them, and the passes and footpaths in the woods were so narrowly watched that it was impossible to obtain even the smallest supply. In this hopeless situation it happened fortunately for them that the Baron *Van Ech*, the governor, died, and was succeeded by M. *J. W. Falk*, a native of Ceylon, a man of much judgment and understanding. He soon after made peace with the emperor, but for which fortunate event the Dutch army, shut up in *Candy*, undoubtedly would to the last man have perished with hunger.—Thus ended a war that had cost the company immense sums of money, and a very great number of troops.

The following morning when we rose, at five o'clock, we found our host sitting under a tree before his door, waiting for us with coffee and a good breakfast. He tried to persuade me to let my companions proceed and to stay with him some days or weeks, assuring me that I should not complain of losing my time. But as I well knew that all the enjoyments he could offer me consisted of good eating and drinking, I thanked him for his kind request, and we left him about seven o'clock, after he had presented us with two bottles of the best arrack of *Batavia,* besides his blessing to accompany us in our journey.

The country through which we now passed lost nothing of its beauty. It was a succession of fine groves and woods, filled with thousands of birds, the singing of which, mixed with the shrill cry of the hazel-hens, which were here very numerous, resounded on every side.

On our arrival at Negombo, we repaired without delay to the commandant, who interrogated us closely respecting our quality, our intentions, the plan of our journey, and the place of our destination. When we had satisfied him, he very politely invited us to his table, for the time we chose to remain, and gave us a large furnished apartment, destined for the accommodation of European travellers, for our abode. There is besides this an ambelam for the Indians, and another for the soldiers and Mestese in the company's service, but they are commonly full, on account of the great passage through this place.

Negombo, which is situated close to the sea, was built by the Portuguese, and taken by the Dutch in 1640. The fort is in good condition, the surrounding country fertile and beautiful, and watered by a broad river, which takes its name from the place. Fresh water and sea fish are in great abundance : and it is here that the most esteemed cinnamon is cultivated. It is said that the ravens contribute greatly to the growth of this tree, from their swallowing a kind of fruit, about the size of an olive, which passes through them undigested, it is therefore strictly forbidden to shoot or kill them. For this reason, incalculable multitudes of these birds are found in Ceylon, the impudence and greediness of which pass all description ; they sometimes fly into apartments which they find open, and carry off every thing that comes in their way. It is not true, as has been asserted, that the fragrance of the cinnamon may be smelled in passing through the woods, as the odour does not spread itself till after the innermost bark, which is the real cinnamon, has been exposed.

The commandant of Negombo showed us great civility, and requested us repeatedly to spend a few days with him and rest ourselves. I should have willingly consented, but the cooper being impatient to reach Colombo, we set out early the next morning. We had now nothing to fear from the wild beasts, as the country was inhabited, free from woods and wildernesses, and interspersed with villages and gardens.

We very soon found ourselves on a fine, broad and level road, planted on both sides with trees, and intersected with gardens of palms, cocoa-trees, villages, country-houses, and detached huts. It is always dangerous to sit bareheaded under the cocoa-trees, as so heavy a nut, falling from such a height, is sufficient to fracture a man's skull, and occasion a most dangerous wound. The cooper having taken off his hat on account of the heat, had nearly loss his life by this means, as the nut in falling grazed his nose.

Having reached the river of Colombo, called by the Dutch, *Groote Pas*, which takes its rise in Adam's Peak,* and falls into the sea a few miles to the north of Colombo, we crossed it by means of a square boat or trough. The small village on the other side, called *Nasigam*, appeared to be populous and flourishing, no doubt on account of the great passage through it, and its vicinity to the capital. At three o'clock we came to a turnpike-gate, where the *dessaronie*† of Colombo commences. Some money was demanded for our passage through it; and after we had taken coffee with the keeper, who was an old invalid serjeant, we slowly continued our journey.

Towards evening we reached a small village, at the entrance of which is situated a country-house belonging to Hock, the *dessare*, or governor of Colombo. The commander of the village, from whom we demanded a lodging, told us, that the ambelam was very full of travellers, and besides, was very small, but that we, by giving a trifling acknowledgment, might pass the night in the governor's country house. We accepted this proposal with much satisfaction. The gardener, who kept the house, opened for us a well-furnished apartment, where we found two beds, which he consented we should make use of.

As the *talwagen*, a sort of arrack, was very cheap here, the baker resolved to avail himself of so excellent an opportunity, and

* Adam's Peak is one of the highest mountains in Ceylon: it lies sixty miles to the north-east of Colombo, and gives rise to three large rivers; the Maliragongo, the largest in the island, which taking a southerly course, flows past Candy, the emperor's capital. The river of Colombo, which runs to the northwest, and the Calitoer, which flows to the south.

This mountain, which is nearly two miles in height, is held in great veneration by the Gentoos and Pagans, on account of a flat stone with the print of a gigantic foot upon it, which they believe to have been Adam's.

† *Dessaronie* signifies *province*, and *dessare* means *governor* of a province.

for that purpose, left the instant supper was over. About an hour after, he was brought back by two koolies, who found him at the door of a surie-shop, so drunk, that he was almost deprived of the use of his tongue, as well as his understanding. Astonished to know how he had contrived to swallow so much liquor in so short a time, we laid him down near us on the sand. Having come to himself a little, we brought him to the house with us, when we were going to bed; but he had no sooner entered the apartment destined for us, than he began to load us with abuse, and laying his hand on his sword, he suddenly drew it out of the sheath, and would certainly have cloven the cooper's head before we could have come to his assistance, had he not lost his balance, and with a tremenduous swing, tumbled between two chairs, where he instantly fell into a profound sleep. He soon, however, began to snore so loud, and in so ludicrous a manner, that we could not forbear laughing.

We got up at break of day, and breakfasted on some excellent coffee. After satisfying the hospitable gardener, we left the house, and at the same time the baker, as we found it impossible to awake him, nor were we sorry at having got rid of him in so easy a manner.

The succession of villages, country-houses, and gardens, with which the road was bordered on both sides; the liquor-shops and casinos, that we met with almost every instant, full of European and Topaze soldiers, indicated our near approach to the capital, Colombo.

CHAPTER X.

Pleasant manner of living at Colombo—Secret longings— MANUEL DE CRUZ*—Singular proposal—Refusal—Salutary advice of the Cooper—Departure from Colombo—Description of the place.*

THE cooper as well as myself had at Colombo many old friends and acquaintance who had established themselves there after the loss of *Nagapatnam.* Among the rest, I may particularly mention Mr. Merlin, a merchant, Mr. Raumer, an engineer, Mr. Beckle, the son in law of my former patron; besides these there were several others. I sent a message to each of these gentlemen informing them of our arrival, and in a very short time they all made their appearance together. It may easily be supposed that the night was spent with the utmost conviviality.

The next day I waited on Mr. *Van der Kegge*, Chamberlain to the *Dessare*, or Governor of the Province, besides several other persons to whom I had letters of introduction. I also visited our fellow traveller, *D'Allemand*, who instead of having met with a friendly reception from the Governor Falk and Mr. Mouncran, was arrested immediately on his arrival. He never would explain the real cause of this treatment, but I afterwards learned that he was suspected of being a spy sent by the English. It is at least certain that something respecting him had been communicated from *Jaffnapatnam*, so that his arrival being expected at Colombo, he was arrested on entering the gates.

As for the cooper and myself, we amused ourselves in the best possible way during our stay at Colombo. We were every day with some of our numerous acquaintances and friends in different parts of the environs of the city, where we amused ourselves at billiards, bowls, and other games. In the evening we were commonly invited to a ball, a party, or a wedding. In this manner we spent a fortnight, during which the Cooper had been flattered with a false hope; but at last he was told that the vacant post he had come to solicit was already disposed of, and given to another.

We therefore began, after the two weeks were expired, to look out for an opportunity of returning to *Jaffnapatnam*. The cooper and myself only were to return, as M. D'Allemand was still in prison, and the baker had had the address to insinuate himself into the favour of a Topaze widow, whose husband had died a short time before, and was just on the point of being married to her. We told him how improper and unlawful it was to marry a sixth wife, while the other five in all probability were still living, but he laughed at our admonitions, and only begged that we would not betray him, which we readily promised, being overjoyed to get so easily rid of him.

The passage by sea was certainly the best and easiest way we could have chosen, but unfortunately the northern monsoon still prevailed in full power. At this season, when the wind is always from the north, and frequently blows very strong gales, the voyage along the coast of Ceylon is very tedious and even dangerous, particularly in the funnies, or other Indian barks, the planks being only sewed together; we, therefore, resolved to make the journey by land, and on foot as we had come, not through the woods and wildernesses, but along the common road, which lies through an inhabited country.

Chance had made me acquainted with my fellow travellers at Jaffnapatnam; and the same chance, or rather misfortune, brought me, during the cooper's illness, into acquaintance with a Portuguese named Manuel de Cruz. He frequented the Inn where we lodged, and often came to drink a bowl of punch with us; he also dined at the *table d'Hote*, or common table.

This man had visited many countries, and there was considerable judgment and correctness in his remarks upon the manners and customs of the various nations through which he had passed. I cultivated his acquaintance with great eagerness, in order to induce him to recount the occurrences of his life, which he said had been very singular and surprising, and to learn what he had met with most worthy of remark in the course of his travels.

When I communicated to him my desire of visiting Candy, the Emperor's capital, and complained of that Prince's severity towards strangers, he observed that this severity was nothing but a political plan to prevent his enemies from becoming acquainted with the passes of his woods and mountains, and did not extend to people of colour, such as Mestese, Topazes, and Malabars, who passed freely through his dominions, either for commercial or other purposes, and that Europeans or whites only, of whatever nation, were prevented from returning. He further informed me that he intended in a short time to set out for Candy. " But," continued he, " I must first accomplish an undertaking in the mountains of *Bocaul,* which I intend to commence as soon as I shall have found a fellow traveller in whom I can place confidence, and such a one is absolutely necessary in an undertaking which will make my fortune as well as his.—I have fixed my choice upon you, because I believe you to be a bold and enterprising person, and one that loves travelling and adventures; but I chiefly give you the preference, because I have an esteem for you, and value your welfare more than that of others."

I begged him to explain his meaning more clearly. After having made a promise of secrecy as he required, he proceeded to inform me that the last time he left Candy with the intention of travelling to *Poetlan,* he had lost his way among the mountains of Bocaul, and while wandering about he had discovered in a deep valley, a small river, at that time almost dry, the banks of which was spread with rubies and other precious stones, but that he durst not carry many of them away, being afraid of falling in with the Emperor's soldiers, who search all strangers that pass near their posts, which spread all over the country. All that he could do was to imprint the spot as deeply as possible in his memory, that he might be able to find it again when an opportunity should occur.

I soon perceived that this undertaking, which he endeavoured to represent as so easy to be accomplished, would on the contrary be accompanied with many dangers and difficulties, not only because he was determined to have only one companion in the expedition, but on account of the necessity of avoiding the beaten paths where the Emperor's soldiers kept watch, and making our way through the lonely and impenetrable forests and thickets which extend to an immense distance behind *Chilau*, and border on those of *Medampe*.

I placed all these difficulties before him in the strongest light, but he used all the arguments he was master of to persuade me to accompany him. I at last requested two days to consider of his proposal, promising him a decisive answer within that time.

I therefore told him that I had resolved to join in the enterprise, on condition that he would allow me to communicate our intentions to the cooper. "The principal objection I have to your plan," continued I, "is, that we two must go alone; this is venturing too much in such wild deserts as we shall have to traverse; I will persuade the cooper to go with us; permit him to join the party; he is a man of courage and enterprise; he suffered much from the English at the taking of Nagapatnam, and is now burdened with a numerous family, whose subsistence is derived from the produce of a small garden he purchased at Jaffnapatnam;—the prospect and hope of enriching himself will perhaps make him joyfully embrace this opportunity. But if he should refuse to accompany us, you may rely upon his discretion; he is a man perfectly honest, and incapable of betraying you, or doing the smallest injury to any man. In a word, it is only on condition that you consent to take a third person with us, that I can resolve to join you in the undertaking."

He then consented, though with evident reluctance, that I should inform the cooper; at the same time declaring, that if he should refuse to go, no other person, not even a kooly, should be permitted to accompany us.

I had flattered myself that the cooper, on account of his family and narrow circumstances, would gladly embrace this opportunity of recovering his fortune; I was therefore a good deal surprised when I saw him shake his head, and smile at my proposal. "Do you think," said he "that such a place would have remained so long undiscovered, when all the other rivers and mines where precious stones are found have been known for so long a period; or that the emperor would not have placed guards there, as well as every where throughout the country? Lay aside, I beseech you, such visionary schemes, and avoid the company of that fool, who, I am afraid, will turn your head with his fortune-making dreams. I depart to-morrow, as you know:—come, let us set out together for Jaffnapatnam.

While he thus held forth against the Eldoradian expedition, the poor Portuguese himself was in the inn, and by chance passed before the glass door of the apartment where we were. The cooper called him in, and severely reproached him for endeavouring to persuade me to so visionary and dangerous an undertaking, and earnestly requested him never to mention it more, unless he chose to force him to take measures which would be by no means advantageous to him.

The Portuguese, disguising his feelings, requested the cooper not to be uneasy, as he had, for several reasons, and after mature deliberation, entirely given up the undertaking, and thought no more of it; on the contrary, he intended to return to the coast of Coromandel, and requested our company as far as Chilau, where, he said he had some business to transact. To this proposal we agreed with great pleasure.

From that moment we began to prepare every thing for our departure. We hired four koolies to carry our baggage, and the most necessary articles, such as arrack, tobacco, &c., besides every thing we did not expect to find in the villages through which we were to pass. It was unnecessary to load ourselves with rice and other provisions, as we had resolved to travel along the coast, which is every where inhabited.

When all was ready, we took leave of our friends and acquaintances, and also of M. D'Allemand, who would gladly have set out with us: he execrated the injustice with which he had been treated, in being thus detained in prison, on account of an unfounded suspicion.

Though it was our intention to depart next day immediately after dinner, we were detained till past five o'clock by other acquaintance coming to take their farewell of us. The koolies, whom we had appointed to meet at one o'clock, finding we did not make our appearance, slunk away, the one after the other, into the casinas, and it was not without great difficulty we found them again. All, however, at last returning, we commenced our march, with a smaller retinue, and less noise, than when we left Jaffnapatnam.

Colombo is situated on the west coast of Ceylon. The harbour is very good for small ships and vessels, but those of burden are obliged to remain in the roads, about a quarter of a mile from the harbour, though they are there exposed to frequent and strong gusts of wind.

This place was taken from the Portuguese by the Dutch, in 1656, after a long siege. The fort has a very fine appearance, and is, in some places, in good repair, but some parts of it are in a very delapidated condition. Several new bastions were constructing when we were there: my friend *Raumer* was the engineer, and had the direction of the works. The Governor, and the principal public official characters reside in the fort. There are very fine streets and houses in it, and it also contains the magazines, arsenals, and counting-houses of the Dutch East India Company.

The city is very pleasantly situated on the side of a fine broad river, full of fish and crocodiles. The streets are very wide, and of considerable length. There are many taverns and coffee-houses, kept in the Dutch manner, where people amuse themselves at billiards, bowls, chess, and other games. The environs of the city are delightful, being composed of avenues of high and umbrageous trees. There are many beautiful walks along the banks of the river, where multitudes amuse themselves, particularly on Sundays, and the suburbs are full of liquor-shops and casinos, which are almost always full of soldiers and the working classes of the people.

The Mestese women of Colombo commonly make use of the Cingalese language, seldom of the Portuguese, and never of the Dutch; instead of shoes they wear *sirrippos*, a sort of wooden sandals; the rest of the body is wrapped round with a piece of linen.

All the provinces of Ceylon, as well as the factories on the opsite coast of Coromandel, are subject to the government at Colombo

CHAPTER XI.

Night of misfortunes—Werigoor—The country after the rainy season—Unpleasant night at Negombo—Disagreement with the cooper—Separation from him—Renewed entreaties of the Portuguese—Consent—Arrival at Chilaw.

IT blew very hard, and the atmosphere was almost entirely covered with clouds. Having passed through the suburbs we entered a broad and level road bordered on both sides with gardens and country houses belonging to the inhabitants of Ceylon. The moon lighted us now and then, through the thick clouds driven swiftly along by the wind.

We had scarcely proceeded an hour on our way when the heavens were again overcast with dark thick clouds, and it very soon began to rain tremendously. Surrounded with thick darkness which did not permit us to see two steps before us, we wandered about in an extensive plain without knowing where we were.

The Koolies began to speak of turning back, but the hope of meeting with some village or grove of trees, drove us onwards. In a short time a broad rivulet appeared before us, and made us suddenly stop. We decided to attempt a passage at once upon the spot where we stood, which was put in execution, and contrary to our expectation, succeeded, the water not reaching higher than our breasts. We recovered the path, and about six o'clock came to a village called Werigoor, situated in a grove of cocoa-trees, half dead with cold and fatigue, drenched to the skin, and covered with mud.

We enquired of an old woman, whom we met on entering the village, if she could prepare any thing for us to eat. She answered that within two hours we should have something that would please us. We gave her money to procure the necessary articles, and in the meantime our people kindled a large fire, before which we dried our wet clothes, and warmed our benumbed limbs. Having taken some coffee and agapés, a sort of cake made of ground rice, for our breakfast, we lay down before the door of the hut, upon some mats spread on the ground round the fire, to recover, in some degree, from our fatigues, the rain having ceased some time before.

When we had dined, we departed, each provided with a Talpat leaf to protect him from the rain, which began to fall anew after we had set out.

Having crossed the river Colombo, we passed through several villages whose names I have forgotten, and of too little consequence to be described.

At mid-day we came to a turnpike gate, where we paid a small toll; there was a Casino here in which we took a hasty dinner. We found ourselves in the evening near Negombo, but from an ill-timed delicacy, we were unwilling to wait upon the Commandant, to avoid which we resolved to pass the night at a small village called Sunampil.

It rained at intervals, so that we found our talpat leaves very useful. Having passed the river Negombo by a small bridge, we kept the town on our left hand, and about eleven o'clock arrived at the village of Toptoore, where we had before been so hospitably entertained by the Roman Catholic priest. I was not a little disappointed when the sexton told us he was gone to Colombo. After dinner, we proceeded along a delightful road, in the finest weather, and towards evening arrived at Ganiepellie, a village situated on the banks of the river Caimelle.

The ambelam was so small, dirty, and ruinous, that we chose to sleep in the open air, rather than be exposed to be bitten by serpents, and venemous insects, which are fond of lodging in the roofs of ruinous huts : the air, on the other hand, was pleasant, and we spread our mats under a large tamarind-tree.

I wished to take up my quarters here for the night, as the weather was so variable, and there was little prospect of falling in with an inhabited place for many miles ;—but the cooper insisted on proceeding immediately, and would scarcely allow himself or us time to take our supper. Seeing that I made no haste to move, but was resolved to remain where I was for the night, he told me roughly, that he would proceed to Jaffnapatnam by himself, and immediately prepared for his departure. His determined obstinacy vexed me exceedingly, and occasioned a warm dispute between us, which rose so high that he at last declared his resolution to travel no longer in my company.

I instantly resolved rather to remain behind and travel by myself, than in company with such a discontented man. I therefore told him that if he chose he might travel night and day, without either eating or drinking, but that I had no desire to perish of hunger and thirst ; my intention was to proceed at my ease, and probably I should arrive at Jaffnapatnam before him, notwithstanding. I therefore took as much linen from our baggage as I deemed necessary, and ordering my koolies to follow the cooper, I paid him the money for which I had hired them at Colombo, requesting him at the same time, to pay them on his arrival, and to take care of my baggage.

A letter from his wife, in which she mentioned her being indisposed, had caused this extreme anxiety to get home. He was a good husband, and loved his wife much, and as she certainly deserved it, I could not blame him for his haste ; but there was no reason that I, who had undertaken this journey for pleasure, should fatigue myself to death. With regard to Anna, I knew she was in very good hands.

Before my passionate fellow-traveller left us, he whispered to me, for heaven's sake, don't be so foolish as to follow the Portuguese in his visionary enterprize. Had I followed his advice, how many dangers and accidents should I have avoided !

No sooner was the cooper gone, than the Portuguese told me with a smiling countenance, that he was overjoyed at his departure, and as I was now free, he hoped I should no longer refuse to accompany him. I replied that he was greatly deceived, the cooper's departure had not produced the least change in my resolution, on the contrary, my intention was to proceed at my leisure to Jaffnapatnam.

On hearing this, he begged I would listen with patience and attention to what he was going to say, as he would explain the real state of the matter without reserve, after which, he had no doubt I should soon change my opinion.

"It is very well known," he continued, "that in the various and repeated invasions of the Portuguese in former times, of the kingdom of Conde-Udda, the emperors concealed their treasures, consisting of pearls, diamonds, gold, &c. in large iron chests, which they caused to be sunk in the river Mavaliagonga, at the place where that stream washes the feet of the mountains that rise behind the capital, and where the Portuguese were never able to subdue them. My father, whose ancestors had accompanied almost all those expeditions against the emperors, knew, from an old tradition in our family, that the Portuguese got possession of one of those chests, but being obliged to retreat in great haste, they concealed it somewhere among the mountains of Bocaul, in a place known only to a few persons, with the intention to return, at the first opportunity, to carry it away; but being driven back by the Dutch, whom the emperor had called in to his assistance, they had never been able to accomplish their purpose. My father, though his death was unexpected, had sufficient time to communicate this, leaving to me an undertaking, which death prevented him from accomplishing in person. What I have told you of a river full of precious stones, is no more true, than that I lost myself in the mountains of Bocaul; it was on purpose, and after mature deliberation, that I went thither; I knew almost the very spot where the chest was to be found, and I hoped to discover it, and be able to break it open. After a long and fruitless search, I saw with indescribable joy, a small river, flowing at the bottom of a valley below me; I hastened to reach it, but how great was my surprize, when I observed the object of my search in the hollow of one of the rocks of which the banks of the river were composed! It was a sort of coffer, or chest, wholly of iron, and put together with so much art, that I could discover neither lock, opening, nor lid. In vain I endeavoured to break it open with stones, all my labour was fruitless. I remarked the place, however, so well, that it is impossible to miss it:—and to go to find it, is the undertaking to which I endeavour to persuade you. I now wait your decision, and I swear to you, by all that is sacred, that by the way which I shall point out to you, we shall have neither soldiers, posts, nor any thing else to fear. You do not believe that I would venture upon such an undertaking myself, if it could not be accomplished, or was attended with too much danger. It is true, we shall have some difficulties to encounter, and we may even meet with some dangers, but to be able to spend the rest of your life in ease and affluence, is it not worth while to encounter the dangers and difficulties of a few days?"

All this sounded well, and was very probable. The circumstance respecting the emperor's treasures being hid in the Mavaliagonga, and other rivers, upon which he founded his story, was known to me, and perfectly true; but the whole affair seemed so romantic, that I could not help sometimes doubting the truth of his narration. I was not, however, the less undecided what to do; on the one hand appeared riches, and an adventurous enterprize; and on the other side Anna, and others of my friends, expecting my arrival with anxious impatience. At last, my want of prudence, and the kind of enterprise, which accorded so well with my inclination, gained me over, and the same night, when the Portuguese began to renew his intreaties, I gave my consent, on condition that he would swear to me, by all that men hold sacred, that his story, in all its circumstances, was true. He immediately assured me of this, with the most solemn oaths, swearing that all he had told me was true, even to the smallest circumstance.

We now agreed to stay a day or two at Chilaw, to provide ourselves with necessaries, and then, without communicating our intentions to the inhabitants, to penetrate at once into the interior. Having decided upon this, we staid in the watch-hut, till next morning, when we set out, and reached Chilaw about midday. We did not enter the town, but took up our quarters in the hut of a Cingalese, about a quarter of a mile from it. I pretended to be ill, and desirous of remaining till next day.

In the mean time, the Portuguese purchased every thing he thought we should be in want of, which he concealed among the bushes, close to where we were to pass.

CHAPTER XII.

Commencement of a dangerous expedition—First occurrence—Continuation of the journey—Arrival at and entrance into the great forest—Difficulties, obstacles, and dangers—Strange sound—The courageous Bear.

At last, the day appointed for our departure appeared; we set out as soon as it was light, and in order to deceive our host, we took the way to the river, as though we intended to cross it at the usual place; but suddenly turning into the thickets, we went round Chilaw, making our way through marshy ground, sometimes covered with bushes, and sometimes full of small thick woods, till we came to the river *Manasseram*. Here the Portuguese drew from under the bushes our ammunition and provisions, consisting of a bag with about twenty pounds of rice; a pair of pistols, powder and shot, two calabashes, one of which contained about three pints of arrack, the other being empty, and destined for fresh water; a small dish of copper, and a plate of the same metal; a packet of sweetmeats; a small axe; twenty fathoms of rope, besides some files and iron crows, and a large bear-skin.

On coming to the river, we saw a young crocodile, which leaped into the water as we approached. As this river was much swollen by the rain, and very rapid, we went along the banks till we found a place where it was not so broad as farther down. Before crossing, we took our dinner under a large tree.

The landscape before us had an extremely wild and desert appearance; a dreary solitude struck the eye on every side. The banks of the river were sandy, and full of pointed rocks; a solitary tree appeared here and there among the bushes that covered the ground; and, at the distance of a mile, the wilderness of *Medundampe*, was seen stretching itself far and wide, to an unknown extent. This desert consists of nothing but very high bushes and thickets, the abode of every description of wild beasts, particularly buffaloes. Great numbers of venemous serpents of a terrific size, inhabit its recesses, so that the boldest hunter dares not venture into them. To the left, on the opposite side of the river, rose a thick wood of old trees, growing very closely together, and full of brambles and reeds.

Dinner being ended, we pulled off our clothes in order to cross the river. The Portuguese requested me to go higher up, about a hundred yards, and to shout with all my might while he was crossing, that I might induce the crocodiles, if any were there, to come towards me. Then taking a part of the baggage upon his head, he reached the other side in safety, the water coming up to his shoulders; he then returned for the rest of our goods. As soon as they were all over, he gave me a signal to cross also, at the same time beginning to shout as loud as he could. I went into the water trembling like a leaf, every moment expecting to be devoured by one of those monsters. I looked anxiously around, holding my naked sword above my head, determined to thrust it down the throat of the first monster that should approach.

While thus occupied, I happened to turn my eyes to the side where the Portuguese, with his face towards me, continued to shout and bawl till he was hoarse,—at the same moment I saw, with horror and amazement, a tiger, attracted no doubt by the shouting, coming out of the wood, slipping from bush to bush, and approaching my companion with its back bent like a cat, when watching a mouse. I instantly made signs to him, but he did not understand what I meant; seeing this, I forgot my own danger and former precaution, and hastened to reach the other side, when I saw the tiger again appear close behind him, and

W. Read Sculp.

A General of the Cingalese Army.

upon the point of making a spring. At this moment I uttered a piercing yell, which startled the monster; it turned round, and looked steadfastly at me: my companion having now observed it, had the presence of mind to leap into the water. The treacherous animal finding himself discovered, durst not approach nearer, but grinning horribly, and showing his large fangs, he went into the wood, turning his head towards us from time to time.

We immediately proceeded on our journey, and in a short time came to the river Chilaw, whose banks we followed; but owing to the sharp-pointed rocks which covered the bed of the river, and the great heat of the sun, we at last left them, and kept along the edge of the wood that lay on our right hand. We found here great plenty of wild fruit-trees; among others, those which produce the palpalam, or milk-fruit, an account of which I have already given.

We soon after observed that the river began to grow narrower, which increased the rapidity of the current; we also saw traces of wild buffaloes, from which we concluded that they frequented this wood; their proper abode being the wilderness of Medundampé, which lay farther to the right.

I have always been equally, if not more afraid of the wild buffaloes than of the elephants; they are untameable and furious animals. When they take it into their heads to attack a man, it is almost impossible to avoid them; whether their rage is excited by any thing of a red colour, to which they have the greatest aversion—by being wounded, or by having been overcome in single combat by a rival; and even should the object of their fury be fortunate enough to reach a tree, and get up into it before the fatal blow be given, he is lost if it happens not to be a fruit-tree, as the animal will not leave the spot till his enemy be in his power, though he should die of hunger at the foot of the tree.

The wood, at this place, was full of small red apes, and various sorts of birds, whose singing and chattering, mixed with the clucking of partridges and hazel hens, resounded through the forest.

Hitherto the river had been bordered, almost to the water's edge, with the trees of the wood that lay on our right hand; but in the evening we came to a place where they retired somewhat, forming a corner of about two hundred paces, consisting of a plain, or open space; the ground was dry and level, and we resolved to pass the night here.

Our first care was to provide ourselves with a good supply of dry wood, which we spread in a semicircle round us, in heaps a few feet distant from each other, the two extremities of the half circle extended to the river, which covered our rear, and served as a place of retreat from danger, if any wild beast had attacked us within our ramparts of fire, which seldom happens.

Having drawn lots which of us should watch for the first three hours, and the Portuguese having the turn, I spread the bear's hide (which served both for our table and bed,) near another fire we had kindled close to the river, and being extremely fatigued, I fell asleep as tranquilly as if I had been in my own house; so true it is that custom reconciles us to any thing.

I slept soundly till my fellow-traveller awoke me to take my turn in watching. He had heard nothing during his watch except the lowing of wild buffaloes, and the heavy tread of some large animals crossing the forest.

As soon as he lay down I stuck my pistols in my belt, laid my gun, loaded with two balls, upon my knee, and having lighted a cegar, I passed the time very quietly; keeping up the fire when it seemed to decrease, from time to time reading and examining my journal, and writing down the occurrences of the preceding day.

Besides a cracking, or loud noise, here and there in the forest, and from time to time the trampling of huge animals crossing the plain on which we had encamped, I heard now and then a sort of blowing, or motion in the river, which I supposed to be occasioned by the crocodiles; but as these amphibious animals are still more afraid of fire than the wild beasts, I was not apprehensive of their visiting us, especially as that side of the river where we were was bordered by a ledge of pointed rocks, and they never come on land except where the ground is sandy and even. This arises from the fear of being wounded in the belly, which is extremely soft and tender, while, on the contrary, their backs are covered with a hard and scaly hide, so thick that neither darts nor balls can penetrate it.

At last day-light appeared. We breakfasted, and then set out, following the banks of the river, which turned its course considerably to the north, so that we very soon lost sight of the desert of Medundampé, which lay behind us.

The wood along the side of which we proceeded, became here beautiful beyond description; trees of a surprising thickness exalted their proud tops, and the thick and interwoven shade permitted the sun's rays to spread only a feeble and melancholy light. Various sorts of birds, many of them unknown to us, hopped about, and perched upon the small branches; their beautifully variegated plumage delighted the eye; and their various notes and cries echoed on every side. Great numbers of small red apes amused themselves by leaping from branch to branch; they redoubled their cries and leaps on our approach, making the most ludicrous gestures and attitudes that can be imagined.

The wood being so delightful, I proposed to my companion to penetrate farther into it, but still to keep the river in sight. A refreshing coolness, and the delicious fragrance of aromatic plants and wild fruits, restored our enfeebled powers. We dined here, under a tree, entirely covered with white flowers, or blossoms, of a pleasant smell; our meal consisted of two red snipes;—a nest of bees, which we found in the hollow of a tree, served us for a dessert.

Having rested a couple of hours, we proceeded on our way. We observed several herds of antelopes, which did not seem to be very wild; and, for the first time since leaving Chilaw, we saw traces of elephants, though not very recent. About five in the evening we came to the place where the river divides itself into two branches, one of which takes its course to the north-east, and the other, which is the larger, runs towards the south-east.

From this place we saw, very plainly, the tops of the mountains of *Bocaul*, behind an immeasurable forest; my companion gave a shout of joy, and pointing to them with his hand, he exclaimed—" soon shall we be at the end of all our difficulties and dangers; two or three days at most, and I shall hear you bless the moment you became acquainted with me." He said many other things to encourage me, to cherish the hope of success in our undertaking, and to dispel the doubts which he thought still arose in my mind.

The sun now set, and we hastened to collect dry wood, to protect us from the elephants and buffaloes, which, from various remarks we had made, seemed to be very numerous in this wood. We fixed our quarters in the angle formed by the bend of the south-east branch of the river, so that we had only to form a quadrant with our heaps of wood, to be protected on all sides; behind us, and on both sides, we were covered by the river and the sharp rocks on its banks, and for greater security, I set fire to the trunk of an old withered tree, a few paces from us, which soon produced a great and brilliant flame. This, joined to the light of the fires that surrounded us, illumined all the plain, and the forest to a great distance.

We spent the greater part of the night in tranquillity, though we heard on the right and left a great noise in the river, besides the snorting of buffaloes, which probably were washing themselves in the water.

About three o'clock in the morning I all at once heard the trampling of animals, running directly towards us, and almost at the same instant saw a tiger pursuing a deer at full speed; the poor animal shot past our fires like a flash of lightning, and threw itself into the river to reach the other side, where it would be safe from the pursuit of its unrelenting enemy. On seeing us the tiger suddenly stood still, but having looked at us for some time with glaring eyes, he fled, howling, into the forest. I had awoke my companion on hearing the noise, and we stood with our guns pointed at him, and ready to fire. The birds soon after announced the approach of day, and we resumed our journey with renewed vigour.

We now crossed the south-east branch of the river, and entered a sandy plain, which extended to the wood that lay about three miles before us. We were now, to our extreme regret, obliged to leave the river, and for the last time we filled our calabashes with its clear and refreshing water. We now supposed we were about twenty miles from Chilaw, which was certainly no great distance in two days, but being heavily laden we could not travel quickly.

From the time we left Chilaw we had not seen any signs of houses or inhabitants, though the country was very fine, and the land, to all appearance, in general very fertile. Our way now lay through fine and deep sand, where we were greatly exposed to the heat of the sun, the rays darting vertically upon our heads, and, except a few straggling bushes, we saw nothing on our way that offered the least shade, where we might have rested a few minutes. At last, however, covered with sweat and dust, and almost fatigued to death, we arrived at the great forest that bordered the plain, and lay between us and the mountains of Bocaul.

As it was already late, we resolved to remain here all night, and next day to cross the wood, which appeared to be thicker and wilder than that we had left in the morning; we hoped, before the day closed, to reach the foot of the mountains.

Our supper consisted of some talingas we had killed by the way. During the whole night we heard the sorrowful voices of the sloths, which answered one another, interrupted from time to time by the shrieking of night owls and bats, and the howling of jackals.

On entering the wood, we found openings here and there, which made our progress in some degree easier; but in a short time it became so thick that we could not, without great difficulty, make our way through the bushes, thickets, and withered leaves, that covered the ground, and under which the serpents conceal themselves.

After proceeding in this manner for about an hour, we suddenly heard on our right a noise that rapidly approached; from the grumbling sound that accompanied it, we concluded that it could be nothing but a herd of wild swine. I was aware that those animals seldom attack men, except they happen to interrupt their progress when running; without waiting to deliberate, therefore, we instantly threw down our baggage, and, with the help of some branches that hung near the ground, we climbed up into one of the nearest trees.

We had scarcely got up, when a herd of about thirty wild swine passed at a hard trot, taking their course directly under the tree where we sat: as soon as they observed us, they set up a prodigious grunting and squeaking, and ran off in two parties. One of them, the first that ran directly over our baggage, being startled by the large roll of cord which happened to lie in his way, sprung to one side in a most ludicrous manner, but immediately recovering himself, he turned round, and falling furiously upon the roll, carried it several yards between his tusks.

When we thought they had got to a sufficient distance, we came down from the tree, and renewed our difficult journey, taking an easterly direction. A small pocket compass served us for a guide, as it would have been impossible to find our way, or to recover it if lost, among trees whose interwoven tops formed an impenetrable and uninterrupted green vault; or among the bushes with which we were surrounded, which were sometimes so high that we could not see three steps before us.

We were not long in meeting with a fresh incident :—passing by a tree of uncommon thickness, a sound, like the voice of some strange animal, seemed to issue from it, though we could observe no opening; till at last, taking my pistol in my hand, I went round to the other side of the tree, where, to my great surprise, I found that it was hollow, and served as a retreat for a she-bear, which, fortunately for us, was then absent, and that her two cubs in playing together, had caused the sound which appeared so singular. As soon as they observed us, they ran into a corner to hide themselves, where they sat grinning and growling at us. The Portuguese, who, in spite of all my entreaties, was determined to make an end of them, drew his sword to cut them down; when, suddenly, a great movement in the bushes behind us, put us to flight with all speed, expecting every moment to see the old bear at our heels.

After half an hour's walk, we came to a morass covered with weeds from three to four feet high. In order to avoid a great circuit, my companion wished to go directly across it, but knowing that tigers and venemous reptiles frequently haunt such places, I opposed this; he proceeded, notwithstanding, and I followed. We had not however taken ten steps, when the crust with which the heat of the sun had covered the mud gave way and we sank to the knees in it, at the same time a cloud of large insects from among the weeds and bushes, attacked us so quickly that all the exposed parts of our bodies were instantly covered with them, before we could disengage our legs from the mud. Having at last struggled out, we set off at full speed, but those blood-thirsty insects followed us to the wood, and did not leave us before our faces and hands were covered with blisters, by their poisonous bites.

It was not without great difficulty, we got round this morass, accompanied by the thickets that covered its sides, and the disagreeable smell, at the places where the surface had no crust upon it.

Having reached the other side, we saw, at a little distance, two bears, one of which was ascending a tree, while the other went round it, and appeared to keep watch. As soon as they observed us, the one in the tree instantly came down, and took to flight, but the other, more courageous, stood still, growling at us, and showing his teeth.

"I believe this beast is resolved to fight us," said I to my companion; "let us see what his intention is, or rather, let us make a small circuit to avoid him." He laughed at my fear.—"If it were an elephant, or buffalo," replied he, "I should agree with you, but to run away from a bear, would be a disgrace; you shall see how I'll make him leap."

Upon this he advanced, shouting with all his might, and swearing at the beast, in the Cingalese language; but he soon changed his tone, upon finding that the bear, instead of running away, advanced upon us, with large strides.—*Maria es ta vi!* he exclaimed, and in a moment, throwing down our baggage, we took up our guns, and fixing the bayonets, posted ourselves behind two large trees; we instantly agreed not to fire, till the bear was within reach of our balls, and then only the one after the other, that we might have time to load again.

Scarcely had we hallooed out this to each other, when I saw the bear about ten paces from me, roaring dreadfully. I fired, and was fortunate enough to shatter his right paw; he fell upon his nose, but instantly recovering himself, he ran upon his hind legs, towards the Portuguese, behind whom I had retired to load again; he fired but missed, when, instead of presenting his bayonet or firing his pistol, he took shelter behind another tree: the bear still following him, I sent a ball into his side, upon which, foaming with rage, he began to howl and roar in a frightful manner, and placing his sound fore foot against a tree, he stood still.

We supposed he had now become weak, and watched the moment of his fall; when suddenly, giving a tremendous roar, he flew at us like a dart, and came so quickly upon me, that I had just time to draw my sword and plunge it to the hilt in his belly, at the moment when he stretched out his paw to seize my arm. I left the weapon in his body, but he drew it out of the wound with his teeth, gnawing it with rage; then, struggling upon the ground, soon expired under our blows.

Without giving ourselves more trouble with our adversary, I cut off one of his ears as a token of my victory, and we left the field of battle as soon as possible. The fear of a visit from bears, and the desire of getting to the end of our journey, made us proceed with more than usual expedition.

The bears of Ceylon are neither so large nor so savage as those of the north of Europe; it seldom happens that men are attacked by them, unless it be a she-bear afraid of losing her young. The one that attacked us with so much rage and fury, seemed to suppose that we wished to discover his retreat, whither, no doubt, the female had fled, for whose protection and his family's he had so courageously sacrificed himself.

We made a circuit to avoid the place towards which the she-bear had retreated; and went on with anxiety and circumspection, being afraid of disturbing or falling in with some other wild beast. Having come to the side of a pool of muddy water, we sat down to rest from our fatigue; after which we refreshed ourselves with a good draught of arrack, and filled our calabashes with the muddy water, lest we should not fall in with any other.

CHAPTER XIII.

Difficulties increased—Perilous night—Inauspicious prosecution of our journey—The tiger's den.—Unforeseen obstacles.

THE farther we now advanced, the wood became the more impenetrable. The ground was covered very thick with thorns, thistles, and weeds, and we were frequently obliged to make a circuit of twenty or thirty yards in order to advance six or seven. Thick old trunks of fallen trees, hollowed by time and overgrown with a covering of woodbine, often fell in our way and obliged us to look for another path: we saw some that appeared quite fresh, though they consisted of nothing but bark, the inside being quite reduced to dust, into which sometimes half our bodies sunk, in endeavouring to get over them. Add to this the hills raised by the Vaios, or white ants, some of which were from four to five feet in height; and the woodbine, which sometimes formed an impenetrable wall. We also suffered much from the red or fire-ants, which fell upon us, and although we covered our faces and hands with handkerchiefs, the bites raised a blister like that occasioned by the sting of a nettle. But the greatest obstacle to our progress was a sort of creeping tendril, or ground ivy, which shot along the ground in every direction, and sometimes held us as fast as if we had been taken in a net or gin; they were full of sharp thorns, which tore and wounded our clothes and limbs very severely. The fruit, however, was of considerable service to us; it was about the size and shape of an olive, and of a grey colour; under a fine scaly shell it contained a bluish substance, of an acid taste and very refreshing. We provided ourselves with a large supply of this fruit, as our water began to fail, and we were uncertain of finding any.

After two hours of hard and difficult labour we at last came to a large pond of muddy stagnant water. We were half dead with fatigue, our arms and faces covered with red blisters, and our legs torn and bloody. We resolved to stay here all night on account of the water being so near; it was however so dirty that we were obliged to strain it through a cloth; what still remained in our calabashes, we preserved to quench our thirst, and did not touch it as long as any of the fruit we had gathered remained.

We had scarcely sufficient strength remaining to collect some dry wood and prepare our supper. Having somewhat recovered from the fatigues of the day, I began to converse with my companion about our situation and circumstances, and the small probability of our reaching the mountains the next day, if, which we had reason to believe, the wood should continue as wild and impenetrable. He laughed at my apprehensions, and did his best to assume a cheerful appearance, though his anxiety was probably greater than mine. "The forest must certainly become more open and passable as we approach the mountains," said he, "and at the worst, it is only one more disagreeable day: we are now too far advanced to think of returning; take courage, my friend, the end will crown the work, and I have reason to hope, the fatigues and privations we now suffer will be richly rewarded."

I was silent—what could I answer him. I was ashamed to show less courage than he, but I repented, with all my heart, having involved myself in so many unnecessary difficulties; and, notwithstanding all he said to persuade me to the contrary, I felt but too well, that a journey so difficult as this was, would in less than three days overcome our strength, in which case we had nothing to expect but a tragical end to our undertaking.

I had imagined that there were few wild beasts in this wood, but I was deceived;—no sooner had night covered those dark, sad, and solitary regions, than we heard, not only the roaring of tigers, but the barking of jackals, with the cries of other animals.

The noise in a short time increased, and approached nearer and nearer, and very soon we saw, by the light of our fires, the performers make their appearance among the trees. Their numbers increased every moment, and one would have thought that all the monsters of the wood had assembled to make a general attack upon us. Soon becoming bolder, they approached our fires, and at last completely surrounded us. The noise and uproar they made were truly terrific. Their hideous roars and cries, mingled with the lamentable howling of the jackals, resounded through the forest, and filled us with terror and anxiety.

It was not difficult to discover that we had brought ourselves into this disagreeable and dangerous situation, by taking up our quarters at the side of the pool, which prevented the animals from drinking. The ravenous and other animals commonly remain in their dens and holes, during the day, and it is only at night they leave them to seek for prey, or quench their thirst. Water is extremely scarce in these thick woods, and sometimes in a circuit of several miles, none is to be fouud, but a few pools filled by the rain, the water of which, in the dry season, is daily diminished by the heat of the sun, as well as by the numerous drinkers. There was probably no other in the neighbourhood besides the one we had taken possession of, it was not therefore surprising that so many heated and thirsty animals should become furious at being denied access to their only resource. We would, however, have gladly allowed them to pass, if it had been possible to take refuge in a tree without leaving our fires, or running the risk of being torn in pieces before we could reach one.

Our fear was now indescribable, for two tigers, bolder than the rest, came forward with measured steps, followed by a crowd of other animals, among which were several bears. The two presumptuous beasts coming close up to our fires, stood still and looked at us for some time with glaring eyes, and grinding their teeth in a horrible manner.—All at once, raising their heads into the air, they set up so tremendous a *duo*, that we almost sunk down with terror, and were scarcely able to hold our weapons in our trembling hands, imagining this roar could be nothing else than the signal for a general attack, especially as it was answered by all the other monsters.—In fact, our situation was such as would have filled the bravest heart with terror.

At last one of the tigers came so near that he could have reached us at one leap. I snatched the thick end of a burning branch from the fire, and hit him so exactly upon the nose, that he tumbled over, staggered about in such a laughable manner, as in any other circumstances would have afforded us considerable amusement. He too k to flight at full speed, and his companion retired soon after; they were, however, succeeded by others from time to time, and even the jackals were not afraid to show themselves. These animals continued all night round our fires, and it was only by firing our pistols, and throwing burning pieces of wood, that we kept them in terror, and at a proper distance.

At last the shades of night began to disappear by degrees, and our enemies along with them; they retired one after another, into the recesses of the forest: their roaring was only heard at a distance, and we thanked heaven for having preserved us in the midst of such danger. After refreshing ourselves, we re-commenced our painful journey, although almost overcome with fatigue and want of sleep.

We had the same difficulties and obstacles to struggle with as before;—heavily laden and fatigued as we were, we made but little progress, and were obliged to stop and rest ourselves at every movement. We struggled in this manner among the high bushes that surrounded us till nine o'clock, when, finding it impossible to proceed, I made my companion halt. "I must sleep a little," said I; "you must however keep watch, and when my strength is somewhat restored, we will continue our journey." Without waiting for his answer, I threw myself on the ground and instantly fell into a deep sleep.

I might have slept about two hours, when my companion awoke me, saying that he would have allowed me to sleep some time longer had it not been for a tiger that had disturbed him for more than a quarter of an hour, and kept walking round and lurking sometimes behind one bush, sometimes another, waiting only for an opportunity to fall upon us. I started up, and seeing him about twenty paces from us, lurking behind a bush, we leaned our guns against the trunk of a tree, and fired at the same time. He sprang several feet from the ground, and instantly falling again, we heard him struggling with the agonies of death. We were so low spirited, and fatigue had rendered us so languid, that we had not even the curiosity to go and look after him; on the contrary, we took up our burdens and resumed our sad solitary way. I am persuaded that the sound of our copper dish, which we beat upon from time to time, contributed not a little to our so fortunately escaping death.

Some time after we observed that the wood, which had hitherto been impenetrable by the sun's rays, began to be somewhat thinner and lighter, though it became closer and thicker under our feet. The trees, however, diminished insensibly, and very soon we had no more trouble from the thorny ground plants and creepers, nor the red ants; and the woodbine did not obstruct our progress; but instead of all this, our heads were exposed to the burning rays of the sun; and obstacles still more difficult to overcome stood in our way.

The tall weeds and bushes increased so much, and became so close, that at last nothing was to be seen but an immense field of high thickets, extending as far as the eye could reach, and only bounded by the mountains of Bocaul, that now appeared at the distance of three or four miles, according to our calculation, which, however, was very uncertain, as we had supposed them to be at nearly the same distance two days before.

We were to find our way through these thickets, on the tops of which it seemed less difficult to walk, than to force a passage. We wandered about as in a labyrinth, and were often so encircled that we had the greatest difficulty to find the place through which we had struggled a few moments before; it was impossible to see three steps before us, from the height of the shrubs and bushes, being much taller than a man. Had we fallen in here with a tiger, feeble and powerless as we were, and without a tree to take shelter in, our chance of escaping would have been but small. I cursed my credulity and foolish curiosity, which had brought me into such circumstances.

With the compass in my hand, I endeavoured to find a passage, but we often came out near the same place, and sometimes farther back than before; add to all this, a deep and burning sand, into which we sank to the ancles, and traces left of serpents that had crept over its surface, were frequently visible, as well as the footsteps of tigers and other animals.

The weather, which had hitherto been delightfully dry and fine, now changed to rain, which soon began to fall very heavily: this was of some service to us, as it cooled the air and the ground, and the clouds intercepted the rays of the sun.

Having come to a solitary tree, we sat down under it to rest ourselves, as its thick foliage protected us from the rain. We had not been long here, when a great commotion took place in the tree; and upon looking up we saw a tiger-cat, disturbed by our presence, springing from branch to branch; sometimes she ran up to the top, and then descended close to us. I could perceive she was preparing to spring at our heads, for the tiger-cat of the east is often more to be feared than the tiger himself, especially when confined, or hard pressed by an enemy. We therefore removed to a little distance, to let her come down, which she did at three leaps.

As the day was far advanced, and the tree under which we sat was very high, and the foliage very thick, we resolved to pass the night among its branches. Sad necessity obliged us to have recourse to this, the bushes being so close that it would have been impossible to make a circle of fires wide enough to hold us in the middle, without being scorched to death; besides, we could scarcely find dry wood sufficient to boil our rice, much less to keep up several large fires during the whole night. The rope we had brought with us was now of great service; we wove it between two large branches like a net, upon which we could lie without being in danger of falling, and in order to prevent it from hurting us, we covered it over with leaves and twigs. Not being certain if we could reach the foot of the mountains the following day, we made ready a sufficient quantity of rice for our next day's dinner.

As soon as it began to grow dark, we hung our luggage upon a branch, and ascended to our elevated couch, in which we placed ourselves, as well as the narrow limits would permit, and rather in an uneasy, half-sitting posture it is true, but it had the advantage of being tolerably secure. We smoked our cegars with a certain sort of satisfaction, and the idea of being secure from danger made us take a pleasure in listening to the cries of the various night-birds and wild beasts which surrounded us. A movement that we heard from time to time above our heads, made us conclude that we were not the only inhabitants of the tree, notwithstanding the two pistol-shots we had fired before ascending it.

The cackling of hazel-hens, and the cries of the wood-ravens had no sooner announced the break of day, than we left our retreat, where we had passed a tolerably quiet night. Having cleaned our arms, and taken down our rope from the tree, we ate the rest of our rice, and refreshed ourselves with a good draught of arrack. The first rays of the sun gilded the tops of the Bocaul mountains, which now appeared very plainly at a short distance. This sight re-animated our courage, and we began our journey with renewed zeal and vigour, fully persuaded that before the evening we should arrive at the foot of these mountains. Notwithstanding all our efforts we proceeded but slowly, on account of the circuits we were often obliged to make, in order to find a passage through the shrubs and thickets.

After proceeding about an hour, a disagreeable smell among the bushes, like that of a dead carcase, made us apprehensive of being near the abode of a tiger, or other wild beast. With our guns ready loaded in our hands, we endeavoured to avoid the spot whence the smell seemed to proceed, but after going on for a quarter of an hour it still appeared to grow stronger, and we found ourselves so completely shut in by the bushes and shrubs, that it was impossible to know from what side it came. Afraid of suddenly falling in with the abode of some monster, while endeavouring to avoid it, we resolved to proceed right forward, with our guns ready cocked, and pistols loaded. Scarcely had we advanced a few steps through a small opening, when, to our great surprise, we saw stretched upon the ground, near each other, the carcases of a tiger and a bear, already half-consumed by the ants which fed upon them. At a little distance we found the tiger's abode, indicated by the bones of her prey, and the skeletons of her young ones. The bear had probably by chance approached the retreat of the tiger, which had fallen upon him, and the fight had ended fatally for both combatants. We left the spot with all the speed we could make use of, which was not great, on account of the close thickets.

About eleven o'clock we found it impossible to proceed farther; the deepness and heat of the sand, the labour of forcing a passage through brambles and thickets, and the scorching rays of the sun, had so overcome us, that we threw ourselves down at the foot of a tree that happened to be near. It was fortunate we had prepared a double portion of rice the evening before, otherwise we should have been unable to make it ready, or even to collect wood to boil it. After eating some rice, we slept an hour by turns, and then set out, still hoping to reach before sun-set the long-wished for mountains of Bocaul, which now appeared to be about two miles distant. The ground had now become harder, and more stoney, and the bushes were less close and thinner, while the trees began to grow more numerous in proportion. We were soon able to proceed without being obliged to make large circuits, and the trees, which we knew by the bark to be ebony, increased so much, that, about five o'clock, we found ourselves once more in a forest. There were no fruit-trees, and in consequence, few birds; the ground was tolerably free from bushes, and there seemed to be few wild beasts.

We found by the way a pool of tolerably clear water, our great want of which overcame the antipathy occasioned by multitudes of small red serpents, about three inches long, and the thickness of a large nail, that were swimming about in it. We concluded they were too small to be venemous, and, therefore, straining the water through a cloth, we filled our calabashes, without any fear of the consequences.

As we proceeded without interruption, we approached the mountains very fast, when we suddenly found our progress obstructed by a canal, or ditch, upwards of thirty feet wide, and, to all appearance, very deep, which lay directly across our path, and stretched to the right and left, as far as the eye could reach.

CHAPTER XIV.

Fruitless efforts to effect a Passage—Desperate attempts—Lamentable end of the Portuguese—Melancholy reflections.

CONFOUNDED at so sudden an interruption, when we thought

ourselves so near the accomplishment of our expedition, we looked at each other without being able to utter a word.—A deep silence prevailed for some time, but at last recovering our spirits, I said that nothing remained to be done, but to follow the banks of this canal to the right or left, as it must terminate somewhere. I wished to take to the right, which would have brought us to the source, but my companion persuaded me to proceed to the left for some time, and if no opening should appear, to return.

The farther we proceeded, the broader it became, and night at last coming on, we were obliged to halt. The canal, on whose banks we had taken up our quarters, defended our rear, while three fires we had kindled, protected us in front; we were, therefore, sufficiently secure from attacks, and the more so, as besides this, there was a tree in the centre, in which we might have taken refuge. Except now and then the grumbling of tigers, nothing disturbed us during the night.

As soon as daylight appeared we proceeded, still following the bed of the river, till about nine o'clock, when we found that the farther we descended, the broader and deeper it became, and equally impassable as it had hitherto been;—the banks on both sides were high, rough, and almost perpendicular. We, therefore, returned to seek a passage higher up, and proceeded slowly, filled with anxious and melancholy thoughts, not that we despaired of getting over this detestable ditch, but because we should be two or three days later in reaching the place of our destination.

About one o'clock we came, fatigued and covered with dust, to a large tree, which grew close to the side of the abyss. We stopped here to eat our dinner, during which my companion was very pensive and full of thought, appearing to have some project in his head. When dinner was over, he told me with a smiling countenance, that he had discovered a method of getting over without losing our time. His plan was this:—the tree under which we sat was, by chance, exactly opposite to another on the other side; these two trees extended over the canal their thick and long branches, which approached to about fifteen or twenty feet of each other. His intention was to get down into the bed of the river, among the bushes, and cut his way through them with an axe; and when he had got to the other side, I was to fasten our rope to a ramrod, and shoot it over, when he would make it fast to his tree, while I fastened the other end to mine, though somewhat higher; by this means it would be easy for me to descend to the other side with the baggage.

There was but one objection to this plan, which was the impossibility for him to penetrate the terrible mass of weeds, bushes, and brambles. He proposed to wrap up his hands and face with handkerchiefs, leaving only a small opening for his eyes;—"And as I," said he, "have involved you in all these difficulties, it is but just that I run the greatest risk and endeavour to help you out of them." Finding him resolved, I gave my consent, on condition that if he found the attempt too difficult, he should return rather than expose himself to danger.

Having taken a hearty draught of arrack, he began to penetrate this dreadful chaos, upon his hands and knees, while I struck the copper dishes against each other with all my might, to drive away the venomous reptiles. Before he commenced, we threw several heavy stones in the abyss, but the mass was so thick that they probably did not reach the bottom. I proposed to fasten the rope round his body, that by keeping hold of the other, I might draw him out if necessary, but he thought it would do more harm than good, and might hinder his progress by getting entangled among the roots and thorns.

He laboured a considerable time before I lost sight of him, but at last he disappeared, and I sat down on the edge of the abyss, and kept my eyes anxiously fixed, for about half an hour, on the opposite side, expecting to see him emerge from the thickets. All at once I observed an unusual movement among the bushes, accompanied with piercing cries and horrible yells of my poor companion, which I mechanically repeated. That he was in danger admitted not a moment's doubt, but how could I assist him? overcome with despair, I fired my pistols, beat upon the copper plates, run here and there like a madman, and rushing to the place where he had entered, I listened with the greatest attention, but an awful silence prevailing, I burst out into loud lamentations, and called upon my companion by the tenderest names.

Till late in the afternoon I continued my endeavours to help my unfortunate companion, at least to let him know, if he still lived, that I had not departed; I even ventured several yards into the opening he had made, but at last finding that all was in vain, overcome with fatigue, hoarse with shouting, and scorched by the heat of the sun, I sat down at the foot of the tree, lamenting over the situation into which I had brought myself. I soon, however, began to think of means of extricating myself from the adverse circumstances in which I was involved.

I did not hesitate long about the road I should take; to return to Chilaw through the wilderness, by the way we had come, was to expose myself to almost certain death: I shuddered at the recollection of the difficulties and dangers we had struggled with, and wishing to profit by the remainder of the day to leave this fatal place, I got up and made every thing ready for my departure.

I felt an indescribable reluctance to leave my unfortunate fellow-traveller; it seemed as if I was going to leave a part of myself behind me, so true it is, that nothing binds mankind more to one another than suffering misfortunes and hardships together; and their attachment is the stronger according to the mutual services their situation requires. Casting a last glance at the fatal spot where my unfortunate friend had disappeared, I departed, my heart overwhelmed with sorrow. I proceeded slowly along the banks of the canal, bending under the weight of what I was obliged to carry for my support and protection.

A noise on the other side of the canal awoke me from the sad reflections into which I had fallen, and I cast a mournful and spiritless glance upon the surrounding objects. The wilderness seemed doubly solitary, and the want of a companion almost insupportable. The fatal canal, or dried up river, which I continued to follow, was still equally broad, and filled to the edge with an impenetrable mass of underwood of every description.

As the sun had almost gone down, I resolved, for want of a better lodging, to pass the night under a withered tree I found by the way. My first care was to ascend it and break off a sufficiency of dry wood, which kept me occupied till night had cast her dark veil over these dreary solitudes. I immediately kindled my fire to prepare supper, having eaten nothing the whole day; and being still too fatigued to procure game, I was obliged to content myself with rice mixed with water and pepper.

The day having changed to a night of pitchy darkness, my solitary reflections became doubly horrible; what frightful ideas rose in my imagination! My solitary meal was scarcely finished, when the roaring of the wild beasts, which hitherto appeared at a distance, increased so much around me, that I was obliged to take shelter in the tree. Having seated myself across a thick branch, I took the precaution to fasten my arms firmly to another, against which my back leaned, and hanging my gun upon a bough, I committed myself to the Divine protection, and extreme fatigue soon closed my weary eyelids.

CHAPTER XV.

The horned Spider—the Storm—Terrible awaking—Continuation of the journey—Reviving prospects—Hopeless situation.

It was eleven o'clock when I awoke; the sun darted his beams vertically upon my head, a burning thirst consumed me, and I felt an acute pain in my back and limbs, occasioned by the uneasy and unnatural position in which I had remained so many hours. Having descended from the tree, I observed with surprise that the remainder of my boiled rice, which I had been obliged to abandon in haste, had disappeared. A jackal, or perhaps a serpent, had no doubt become master of it; fortunately, I had hung the rest of my rice upon a branch of the tree.

Having quenched my burning thirst, I took up my load and began my march; a severe pain in every limb, and a scorching sun, from which I had not the least shelter, retarded my progress, and rendered it difficult beyond description. At last I came to a pool of water, I sat down to rest a little, and fill my calabash. As it was only two o'clock, I resolved to proceed till four, and then to prepare my dinner, hoping by that time to reach the foot of the mountains, which I calculated to be about a mile distant.

On getting up to pursue my journey, I perceived at my feet an hideous insect I had often heard mentioned, the horned spider. Though I had all my life had a particular aversion to those sorts of insects, curiosity induced me to examine it closely. Its brown rough body was more than six inches round, and its claws, which were about the thickness of a quill, held a lizard, the flesh of which it was greedily devouring. I could plainly see its fiery eyes rolling in its head; and taking a small twig, I held it under its nose, when it instantly darted at it like lightning: letting fall the twig, I set off as if a serpent had pursued me.

I continued my solitary way covered with dust, which filled my throat and nostrils, and occasioned an insupportable thirst. The day had been unusually hot and sultry, which made me apprehensive of an approaching storm.—I was not deceived. Black and copper-coloured clouds heaped upon one another, slowly approached in terrible array, and began to cast a thick and dark veil over the bright azure of the heavens; they seemed to retain with difficulty the lightning and rain with which they were surcharged; the sun was soon overcast, and they already extended themselves over the forest that lay on my right.

The fear of being overtaken by the storm, before my supper and bed were prepared, now changed to the hope of the weather clearing up, as the black clouds which gave me so much uneasiness appeared to remain stationary; and, notwithstanding the continual flashes of lightning that illumined their copper-coloured edges, I heard the thunder at a great distance, and only at intervals. Fortunately the dead trunk of a fallen tree happened to be a few paces distant; I immediately set it on fire, as all the dry wood I could collect was not sufficint to keep up the fire during the night. I then hung my provisions upon a branch of the tree, climbed up, and committed myself to the protection of Providence. What a dreadful spectre struck my sight! The heavens seemed all on fire, and the thick darkness was every moment changed to the brightest day; my eyes were dazzled by the glaring flashes, that rushed from every point of the sky, and were instantly succeeded by an awful peal, that rolled from one side of the horizon to the other. I was obliged to hold one hand to my face to prevent my nose and mouth from being filled with sand and dust, which was whirled round by the wind, and enveloped me like a thick cloud.

At last the tempest began to calm by degrees. Wet to the skin, and shaking with fatigue and want of sleep, I impatiently waited for the dawn, the more so, as I heard a noise at the foot of the tree. In vain I tried to penetrate the darkness, and the rain, which fell at intervals, to discover what animal disturbed me. I had flattered myself that few wild beasts were to be found in this place, as, during the time I had been alone, I had seen none except two bears on the other side of the canal, and some herds of wild swine. The noise continued long, and gave me much uneasiness, but at last it ceased as day-light began to appear.

On coming down from the tree, I observed with regret that the rain had made my rice quite wet, and was much afraid that it would be spoiled if the wet weather continued. Having cleaned my arms, I continued my journey, this being the best method of warming myself, as well as bringing my misfortunes to an end.

I had not proceeded far when I observed at a distance that the wood, which bordered the canal, suddenly turned to the east, and seemed to shut me in. I now concluded that my last hope of deliverance had vanished. "Gracious heaven!" cried I, "what shall I do, if this cursed canal should run through this impenetrable forest, which is full of ravenous beasts, against whose attacks I shall soon be too feeble to defend myself? or should I escape them I must wander about till I perish with hunger and fatigue." I should not have remained in this uncertainty, if a thin mist, hat rested on the tops of the trees and bushes, had not prevented me from seeing that the canal changed its direction with the wood; I observed this when about half a mile from the place where the turn commenced. This place was full of rocks, behind which a chain of mountains raised their bare tops. The liveliest joy now succeeded the sadness and despair which had so long possessed my heart. "Heaven be praised," I joyfully exclaimed, "perhaps I am now at the end of my miseries; I am now near those so long wished-for mountains, and no obstacle seems to prevent my reaching them." I increased my speed as much as my feeble powers would permit, till the beams of the sun, which began to be felt, reminded me of my wet clothes and rice; I therefore kindled a fire, and began to boil my rice.

About eleven o'clock I arrived at the foot of a steep rock, about sixty feet high, and as smooth as a wall, rising like an insurmountable barrier across my path. I looked anxiously about for some time, but no passage or opening appeared. At this frightful prospect my strength gave way, I sunk down upon the earth, and a death-like coldness spread over all my limbs. I remained more than a quarter of an hour in this situation. At length, coming to myself, I gave vent to my feelings in loud and bitter lamentations; I beat my breast, and with terrible execrations, cursed the poor Portuguese, who had already been sufficiently punished for his imprudence.

I spent some time in these useless complaints, till I began to reflect that they only exhausted my remaining strength, and rendered me incapable of getting over those rocks and mountains, if there should be a probability of accomplishing it. I then got up to examine the place more closely, but I was soon convinced that my situation was hopeless; on the left I had the canal, whose banks, from the elevation of the ground, had become exceedingly steep and high, and its bed still exhibited the same solid mass of brambles, thorns, and weeds. Before me was a ridge of rocks, which on the one side overhung the fatal abyss, and on the other extended far into the wood, thus completely shutting in the small space of ground that lay between them. The face of the rock exhibited every where the same smooth appearance, and was as perpendicular as a wall. The only place that an ape, or other climbing animal could have ascended by, was above the canal, where the rock sloped down to the bushes, and was not quite so steep as elsewhere; it was also more or less provided with clefts and holes; but the bare idea of hanging over this gulf, into which the least false step would have plunged me, made me tremble; besides, I should have been obliged to leave my gun and provisions behind me, if I had ventured upon the undertaking.

CHAPTER XVI.

The Pambou-Rajah, or Royal Serpent—Adventrous leap—Singular preservation—Cheerless prospects—Strange Sounds.

THERE remained, therefore, no other alternative than to follow the direction of the rock into the forest, and to get round it if possible, or to find a place where it was less steep, and the summit more easily attainable. But it would have been almost as easy to pierce the rock itself, as to penetrate the close mass of thorns, bushes, and rank weeds, which, interwoven together in every possible way, prevented all access to the foot of it.

Struggling with disappointment and vexation, I followed the edge of the wood, either to see if there was any means of getting into it, as I hoped, by continuing along the side of it to arrive at its termination, or find a passage through it. Having proceeded back about fifty paces with this intention, I had the satisfaction to observe a small opening, through which, with much labour and difficulty, I penetrated into the wood. Scarcely had I entered it when I heard a loud hissing, and uncommon motion in a large tree that stood some paces from me. With all the speed terror permitted, I flew towards the rock, my eyes glanced hastily over it, but seeing the utter impossibility of reaching its top, despair made me resolve to retrace my steps to the spot where I had lost my unfortunate comrade, and all alone as I was, to return to Chilaw by the way we had come, through so many dangers and difficulties. This desperate resolution seemed at that moment to be the only alternative left me in my hopeless situation.

Without further deliberation, therefore, I made haste to take up my gun and provisions, which I had left on the ground in my flight, when suddenly the same hissing that had driven me so quickly out of the wood, struck my ears—I looked round—a monstrous serpent, of enormous size, was crawling slowly out of the same opening by which I had entered a few moments before, and thus my retreat was cut off on every side. At this sight the earth seemed to open under my feet; I uttered a horrible yell, and courage and hope instantly forsaking me, I stood as if thunderstruck, and could form no resolution,—where could I fly?—where conceal myself? I saw the terrific monster ready to swallow me; I saw his eyes glaring, and his throat swelling with fury.

Shut in on every side, nothing remained but to throw myself into the canal, which was on my left;—before me I had the perpendicular wall of rock; on the right lay the impenetrable mass of brambles and weeds, which extended from the rock along the edge of the forest, and cut off all hope on that side. My situ-

W. Read. Sc.

The Pambourahja or Royal Serpent.

ation was such as is not easily described; those who have been in similar circumstances can alone judge what I felt.

An unconquerable irresolution still made me hesitate, but seeing the hated monster open his immense jaws, and quicken his pace, and now only about a hundred paces from me, I rushed towards that part of the rock that overhung the canal. I made a leap about five feet from the rock, and an equal height from the ground, to lay hold of a cleft with my hand,—it succeeded! But for the threatened danger, which called forth all my strength and agility, I should never have been able to venture, much less to accomplish such a leap. I remained some moments hanging by the hands over the abyss, before I could find any small projection on which to place my feet, and relieve my arms from the weight of my body. During this anxious struggle, I expected every moment to be devoured by the monster; fortunately it was not of the species that crawl upon their tails, with their heads erect, like the *naga*. I made incredible efforts to save my life. By seizing upor every projection, and holding fast by every cleft, I at last reached the edge of the rock, and drew myself to the top.

Being now beyond the reach of the monster that pursued me, I sank down near the edge of the rock; the severe exertions I had made, and the idea of having escaped so narrowly, almost deprived me of breath; every limb shook with a convulsive motion. After remaining for some time in a sort of lethargy, I was roused by the reflection that I had lost all the means I had possessed of prolonging my life. I rose up, though scarce able to stand, and casting my eyes towards the serpent, I saw it busy in devouring my rice, which was contained in a goat-skin bag. After swallowing it, the monster made several circuits round the place, raising up the sand with its long tail, and still continuing the same horrible hissing. At last it departed, entering the forest by the same opening by which it had come out. I gazed with horror upon its enormous body, covered with yellow and black spotted scales; it sometimes raised its terrific head, and crept with a slow and regular motion. It appeared to be about fifty feet long, and its body was considerably thicker than mine.

With unspeakable grief I saw at the same time my gun and pistols lying at the foot of the rock. Without this irreparable loss I should have considered my rencounter with the serpent as a fortunate event. I was, in fact, in a certain sense, indebted to it for my life; having as it were with shut eyes, and not considering what I did, ascended this, to all appearance, insurmountable barrier, the fear of instant death having lent me courage and address. In no other circumstances would I have attempted it; the mere idea would have made me tremble, and deprived me of power to execute it. I examined the objects around me with unspeakable anxiety. What a melancholy prospect presented itself! the place on which I stood was part of a chain of steep rude rocks, rising above one another, and surrounded by a dreadful gulf, in the middle of which the fatal canal wound round the bottom of the broken rocks. Almost petrified with terror at this view, I saw too well that my sufferings were not yet at an end; the wild and dreary scene before me, and the want of means to preserve my life, made me conclude that nothing but a miracle could save it.

The sun was almost set,—the hope that my deliverance might be nearer than I expected, suppressed the melancholy reflections that rose in my mind, and without deliberating longer on what was to be done, I got up, and proceeded in an easterly direction, as fast as the ruggedness of the rocks permitted.

Fortunately I met with water in the clefts and holes, otherwise I must have, after all, been obliged to return to Chilaw by the old route, as it would have been certain death to proceed in such a place without water.

The situation of this dreary region left me no choice as to the course I should take. I hoped that, by going along the valley, through the middle of which the canal wound, I might meet with some opening. I could easily perceive that this detested canal, which continually opposed my passage, was nothing else but the forsaken bed of a river, whose wet and muddy bottom had produced such a mass of weeds, bushes, brambles, and creeping plants of every description.

On the approach of night I sought for a proper place for a shelter, if it should rain. There seemed no reason to be afraid of wild beasts, as it was altogether impossible for them to find any prey among these barren rocks. I sat down at the foot of a rock, which, by the projection of the upper part, formed a sort of vault, or grotto, and searching my pockets I found, to my great joy, the tinder-box, which, fortunately, was not left with the rest of my things. Before lying down, therefore, I set fire to a few handfuls of dry weeds and thorns, to disperse the insects and reptiles that might be thereabouts; then throwing myself on the ground, I gave full vent to my sorrowful reflections.

About midnight I was aroused from my pensive musings by a noise like the barking of dogs, accompanied from time to time by deep and hollow tones that seemed to issue from the mountain on the opposite side of the canal. Before I could collect my terrified fancy sufficiently to judge what it might be, I heard the same sound behind me, but at some distance; there even seemed to be the voices of several persons, who burst into loud fits of laughter, which produced an indescribably awful contrast with the stillness of the night, and the dead silence and solitude of the dreary region. This noise continued several minutes, and sometimes seemed to approach rapidly, and then to retreat with equal swiftness. I rose up,—a sudden thrill ran through all my limbs, and I listened with a beating heart; the deep baying resounded in the distance, in flying haste, and was answered by the echoes of the neighbouring rocks.—Again an awful stillness prevailed. All at once, behind the rock on which I stood, a shrill and horrible yell seemed to arise. The blood froze in my veins; I could withhold no longer.—"I must see what it is," said I, "were it Satan himself!" I armed myself with a large stone, and rushed, half desperate, out of the cavern. At the same moment there issued from behind a rock about ten paces from me, such a mixture of strange sounds, so sharp, so piercing, so horrible and uncommon, that I put my fingers in my ears, unable to withstand the hellish tumult, and retreated in such haste that my head struck against a projection of the rock; my face was instantly covered with blood, and I crept into the farthest corner of the cavern.

I do not believe in ghosts and apparitions, neither am I superstitious, or easily frightened; had this been the case I should never have ventured to traverse the most dreary and solitary part of the Island, almost alone. I feared nothing in these lonely regions but the wild beasts. I intended, at first, not to mention this singular incident, afraid of appearing ridiculous, but since my arrival at Jaffnapatnam, I have received from several credible persons more minute and copious accounts respecting these singular sounds, which confirmed all that I have related above;—that in the mountains, and on the banks of the Maweliegonga, strange noises occur, either from gaseous exhalations, or from contests or currents of wind.* The Cingalese imagine them to be the voices of certain exiled *Rajahasjahs*, or evil spirits, but the vulgar Europeans call them cries of wood devils. The philosophical reader will, however, ascribe them to natural causes, at present untraced.

I heard nothing afterwards except the sound of falling rocks, rolling down the sides of the mountains, and plunging headlong into the gulf below; and the splitting of these might have had some connexion with the noises in question. I passed the remainder of the night in continual anxiety, which banished sleep from my eyes. At last the long-expected dawn appeared, and I proceeded on my tedious journey.

---

* In WOLF's voyages to Ceylon, mention is made of the same sounds; and they seem calculated to alarm even a less credulous traveller than our author, whose belief in dreams, and other superstitions, is part of the vulgar mythology of the Dutch, and all Northern nations.—EDITOR.

CHAPTER XVII.

Dangerous ascent of the mountains—The Serpent—The mist—The precipice—Agreeable discovery.

HAVING been during several days exposed to all the changes of the atmosphere, with no other roof than the sky, and having no refreshing rest, I was so exhausted that I was obliged to stop from time to time to take breath.

About nine o'clock I got out of this accumulation of rocks, and all at once came to the foot of a steep mountain wholly destitute of vegetation. Broad and deep chasms on both sides of me, between which I stood as upon an island, prevented me from going round the mountain, and left me no other alternative than either to ascend it, or turn back. I collected all my strength and began the ascent, which I found extremely difficult. The rocks often gave way in my hands, and losing my balance I was in danger of falling to the bottom. But at last, after incredible labour, I reached the summit.

The prospect on the one side was bounded by steep and bare mountains, and on the other, as far as the eye could reach, I could see only an uninterrupted extent of forests, which was lost among dark thick clouds in the far distant horizon. I looked disconsolately around on this desolate and cheerless prospect. Below me I could see nothing but high precipices, rising out of frightful gulfs, or projecting rocks every moment threatening to fall.

With dismay I found that though the side of the mountain which I had climbed was very steep, yet that by which I should be obliged to descend was infinitely more so, being almost perpendicular, except where the mountain joined the canal and formed part of its banks.

I was diverted from my disagreeable reflections by seeing a serpent of about three feet long and as many inches thick, pursuing a lizard, which endeavoured with all its might to escape: from compassion for the wretched animal I took up a stone, and taking a good aim, killed the serpent. The idea of using it for food instantly occurred to me; I knew well that the most venomous serpents, such as the *Naga*, might be eaten, and were often used as a medicine, so that I found no difficulty of making use of the one I had killed. Having prepared it for being roasted, I kindled a fire of some dry bushes I found here and there among the rocks: hunger made it delicious, and I ate the whole of it.

While I was occupied with my wretched meal on the top of this aerial mountain, small clouds began to assemble, and at last they enveloped me with a dense mist. I hoped that they were only passing clouds and that the sun would soon dispel them, but to my great disappointment they remained, and the mist became so thick that in a short time I could see only a few feet around me.

It appeared impossible to descend the mountain enveloped in darkness, when the least false step would have hurled me headlong from the rocks into the abyss below. There was, however, something so truly horrible in the idea of perishing with hunger and misery on the top of a dreary mountain, that I resolved to make the attempt without waiting till the mists were dispelled. I therefore endeavoured to recollect the places that appeared most eligible for that purpose, where the mountain was less steep, and the rocks afforded any thing like a prospect of sure footing. On approaching the edge of the rock where I was to descend, the frightful view still made me hesitate, and I remained some time in a state of painful indecision, till at length the fear of being overtaken by the storm, which seemed almost ready to burst, urged me to the attempt. Falling on my knees, I commended my soul to the Almighty, and without further delay, or listening to the suggestions of fear, I slid over the edge of the rock. I remained for some time hanging by the hands, and still held fast with a convulsive grasp, but it was too late to return; my hands became fatigued, and I was obliged to descend; every step was the result of mature deliberation, and I never removed one foot or hand till the other was fixed. But, notwithstanding all my precaution, I often laid hold of bushes or weeds whose withered roots gave way in my hand, and sometimes the projections of the rock sunk under my weight, and I remained for some moments hanging by my hands over the gulf, before I could find new footing.

After continuing this painful labour about three quarters of an hour, I found myself all at once clear of the mist, but at the same time saw that I had left the intended straight line in descending, and made almost a quarter of a circle round the side of the mountain, which would have brought me much nearer the abyss. It therefore became necessary to change my course, but the frightful position in which I was, occasioned such a dizziness that I durst not move. So long as the mist had covered my view, I scrambled down without much fear, supposing that I was in the right direction, but seeing myself hanging over a black abyss on the side of a precipitous rock, terror seized my faculties, and I remained almost a quarter of an hour motionless. My heart beat violently and a cold sweat covered my limbs. How gladly would I have returned to the top of the mountain! The moment approached when I should be obliged to let go my hold, and I was so confused as not to have observed that the mist had slowly descended and once more enveloped me. No longer seeing the gul. under me, I began to recover by degrees, and at length recommenced my painful and dangerous labour.

Having continued to descend about a quarter of an hour, I laid hold of a shrub that grew in a cleft of the rock, but what was my terror on finding it give way. Before I had time to seize any thing else, my footing failed, and I fell headlong into the gulf! When I came to myself, I was lying in the valley very near the canal. Fortunately the mountain was not very steep near the bottom, and I had not fallen from a great height, otherwise I must certainly have lost my life; I was, however, considerably bruised.

The love of life directed all my thoughts towards its preservation, and I felt that nothing but determined resolution could extricate me from my present unhappy situation. I resolved, therefore, in place of spending my remaining strength in useless complaints, to venture every thing, and leave nothing unattempted for my deliverance.

With this intention I began to seek a path among the rocks, following the direction of the canal. I had not proceeded far, when I observed a bird on the point of a rock; and crept near and took so good an aim with a stone, that he fell to the ground dead. Rejoicing that I had got something eatable, though it did not seem very delicate, I made haste to collect some dry thorns and kindle a fire; and having roasted the bird as well as I could, I ate it up, after which I felt much better, and my strength began to recover.

After proceeding for some time, I found myself as it were inclosed by a circle of high-pointed rocks, which prevented me from seeing any thing but the way I had come, and the sky above my head. I continued, however, to scramble over them in the hope of meeting with a passage. I made very little progress, and the heat of the sun falling upon the rocks, occasioned a continual thirst; fortunately the rainy season was not quite over, and I found enough of water in the holes of the rocks. In the dry season death would have been inevitable.

The day began to close, and it therefore became necessary to seek a place where I could pass the night, and I soon found one that had some resemblance to a cave. I sat down overcome with despondency. When the last rays of the sun gilded the tops of the mountains, I cast a mournful eye upon the wilderness that surrounded me, and the deepest melancholy took possession of my soul. The awfulness of the place and the time, and the faint hope that remained of my being able to bear up against so many sufferings, filled me with horror.

Night overtook me in the midst of my reflections, and cast

a veil over the surrounding objects, and, shivering with the cold damp of the mist, I crept under the rock that was to serve as a shelter. I should willingly have kindled a fire, but the means were wanting; its absence increased the horror of my situation.

Full of restlessness and anxiety, I stretched myself on the cold surface of the rock, still endeavouring to fall asleep, when by chance putting my hand into my pocket, I felt five cegars that had fallen through a hole into the lining of my coat. I struck a light, and smoked them with a pleasure similar to that afforded by a draught of cold refreshing water to a person parched with thirst. My sombre ideas vanished as I continued to smoke; and whether the enjoyment I felt had calmed my perturbed mind, or the fumes of the tobacco had produced a soporific effect, I fell fast asleep.

CHAPTER XVIII.

Faint ray of hope—Disappointment—Last effort—The canal—The Oedoembo—Deliverance—Manioppoe—Arrival at Poetlan, and Jaffnapatnam—Conclusion.

It was broad day when I awoke; my limbs were bruised and stiff, accompanied with a shivering which made me apprehensive of being seized with a fever; a burning thirst consumed me, and I felt, by my feeble state, that this might probably be the last day of my life, if I should find nothing to restore my exhausted powers. I got up from my hard couch, and having in some degree quenched my parching thirst with some water in the rocks, I proceeded on my toilsome journey, keeping to the east as much as possible.

My progress was very slow, having continually to clamber over high rocks, with incredible difficulty and labour, to which my exhausted strength was unequal; I was, therefore, often obliged to sit down and rest myself. The rays of the sun reflected by the rocks, and the closeness of the place, from the height of the surrounding rocks, occasioned a suffocating and insupportable heat. In vain I endeavoured to find some ground for hope and consolation; courage had altogether abandoned me, and a fatal despondency overpowered my soul.

After losing my unfortunate companion, I was still supported by the hope that every step I took brought me so much nearer home, but the unexpected obstacles I had continually met with, and the probability of my not being able to support the want of food much longer, made me now look for nothing but a certain and inevitable death. I had frequently tried to kill some of the birds of prey that alighted on the top of the rocks, but my weakness prevented me from aiming with sufficient address, and I never succeeded.

The sun had finished half his course, when I suddenly found myself before the canal, whose course I had not been able to follow after descending from the mountain, on account of the rocks that prevented my approach. The joy I felt at first sight of this horrid gulf, was greatly diminished on observing that it was almost two hundred feet below me, and the banks extremely steep. Its bed was still full of thorns and bushes, but I could observe here and there pieces of rock that rose above them, which made me conclude that this mass was not so close and impenetrable as formerly; besides, it no longer occupied the whole breadth of the bed, so that there was space enough to walk on either side.

Seeing the impossibility of descending into the hollow, and scrambling up on the opposite side, I concluded, that the only way left was to climb over some steep rocks, in order to avoid those that formed the head of the canal. I therefore began to scramble over as well as I could, but soon found my progress obstructed by awful abysses, and deep chasms, which I could not look down into without horror. "This is the place," I exclaimed, "where my life and miseries must end together; abandoned, without food, I must close my weary eyes, and suffer the last agonies among these solitary rocks, no human being shall be near, to receive my last sigh, or preserve my body from the birds of prey." After sitting for about half an hour, I rose up to examine more closely, whether there still remained any possibility of extricating myself,—all my labour was in vain, there seemed to be no other way left, but to turn back and follow the course of the canal, till I should find a place where it might be possible to descend into it, and reach the other side.

With this intention, I collected all my remaining strength, to ascend a high rock, from which I could see the course of the canal to a considerable distance;—what were my transports on seeing, at a small distance, the bank fallen in on the side where I was. I scrambled down as fast as my weakness would permit, and hastened to the place, where, to my inexpressible joy, I found that the rubbish had fallen in such a manner, as to render the descent to the middle of the bed quite easy.

In the middle of my career I observed, very near me, a ocdeombo,* a sort of crocodile, or large lizard, which perhaps

* This amphibious animal is called, in the Cingalese language, Talgoin, and has already been described.

being frightened by the noise I made in descending, came out of a cleft in the rocks. At one leap I cleared the place that separated me from it, and caught hold of its long tail at the moment when making its escape among the rocks and stones. I drew it out with considerable difficulty, as it held very fast, and instantly shattered its head against the rock. I arrived at the bottom happier than a monarch, and sitting down to rest, I looked at my booty with inexpressible satisfaction, well knowing its renovating properties.

It began to grow dark. On looking round I observed near me a small, somewhat elevated hollow in a rock, in which I resolved to pass the night. I made haste to collect some withered bushes, and make a fire, after which I prepared my oedoembo. It weighed only about three pounds, but those that are near rivers or fertile places are much heavier, sometimes weighing ten or twelve pounds. I then cut it in small pieces, and my hunger was such, that in a short time I devoured, rather than eat, nearly one half of it.

Having finished my meal, I threw myself on my knees, thanking the Almighty for his goodness in having thus far preserved me from perishing of hunger;—my courage revived, and I put on a determined resolution never again to give way to despair, and to persevere to the last extremity. With the flattering hope of next day seeing an end to all my troubles, and with the consoling idea of possessing the means of existence for at least a day or two, I lay down to sleep without anxiety or fear at finding myself alone at the bottom of this awful gulf; and without being afraid of wild beasts; on the contrary, I slept so sound that it was broad day when I awoke.

Having breakfasted on a few morsels of my oedeombo, and put the remainder in my pockets, I set out, more vigorous than ever, towards the head of the canal. As the bushes were now only in the middle of the bed, I scrambled over upon the rocks that rose here and there above them, and soon found myself on the other side of the mass of thorns, bushes, and weeds, in which my unfortunate companion had lost his life, and so long had denied me a passage.

I now began to run with all my might, like a lost child that sees the well-known dwelling of its parents at a distance, and runs towards it with outstretched arms. I came to a turn, but had so sooner reached it than I stood motionless; in vain I opened my mouth, and made several efforts to utter a sound, my voice died upon my lips, and tears ran down my hollow cheeks.

My transports were occasioned by seeing, in an open place in the wood, a party of Cingalese at dinner, with their oxen grazing around them. They did not observe me at first, but having come to myself a little, the sound of my voice reached them. They were not a little surprised at my appearance, and came towards me with marks of astonishment, but they no sooner approached, than joy overcame my enfeebled faculties, and I sunk upon the ground in a swoon. The good people did all they could to recover me, and at length they succeeded. Being extremely weak and indisposed, they prepared some infusions of plants which threw me into a sound and refreshing sleep.

Next morning, about eight o'clock, they awoke me to proceed on my journey; I had slept almost twenty hours. They set me upon one of the oxen, and I began by degress to be more tranquil and composed. I was in a caravan consisting of twenty-four men, and upwards of fifty loaded oxen. Observing the chief near me, I approached him to offer my acknowledgments, but great was my surprise upon finding him to be no other than the worthy Manioppoe, whom I had met with soon after leaving Jaffnapatnam; he expressed a desire to know what accident had brought me to that place. As it was of the greatest importance to conceal my motive for undertaking the journey with the Portuguese, I told him, that having been on a hunting expedition in company with another Mestese, we were attacked, when on our return, by a wild buffalo, which killed my companion; that in endeavouring to escape I had lost my way, and wandered several days among the mountains without food. Manioppoe informed me in his turn that they had come from Deligieour, and were going to Poetlan to purchase salt. My joy was not a little increased on hearing that his destination was the same as my own. I therefore requested him to allow me to accompany the party to that place, to which he most willingly consented.

We continued our journey without meeting with any thing remarkable, and in three days reached Poetlan, where I took an affectionate farewell of the friendly Manioppoe, and hiring a vessel, in a short time arrived at Jaffnapatnam. I shall say nothing of my meeting with my friend and with Anna, descriptions of such scenes have often been attempted, but they always come far short of the reality. The events of this journey have left an indelible impression upon my mind, they have presented the vicissitudes of life in a new point of view, and I have drawn from them this conclusion. Never to lose courage in any danger, or to despair in any difficulty, however great.

THE END.